THE ART OF FOOD AT

Lucio's

THE ART OF FOOD AT
Lucio's

LUCIO GALLETTO and TIMOTHY FISHER

FOREWORD Leo Schofield   INTRODUCTION Robert Hughes

AND A SALUTE FROM John Olsen

CRAFTSMAN HOUSE
G+B Arts International

Especially for Lucio in appreciation of grand times at his restaurant —

John Olsen Oct 97

contents

Foreword

Some buildings are cursed. Scenes of serial bad experiences, they feel doomed. Others are blessed in their sequence of occupants, happy buildings that wear a perennial smile and seem always to radiate a kind of benign glow. One such is the Victorian building at the corner of the regally named Windsor and Elizabeth streets in Paddington.

It resembles a hundred other such buildings scattered through the older quarters of Sydney, set square to each street with a canted corner for the entrance door and stoop and a verandah of dished corrugated iron over a pretty cantilevered balcony trimmed with iron lace that provided both shade for the two shop windows below, now enlarged, and a cool place for sitting out on summer evenings. By way of additional ornament, a row of cast cement balusters and vases crowns the façade, lending the building an Italianate air. In its first incarnation it must have been a corner shop, perhaps one of the general stores of which there were examples on almost every corner in this part of town.

At the time of the first wave of Paddington gentrification in the early 1960s, the admired cook Madeline Thurston, a kind of Antipodean Elizabeth David, leased the building. She lived above and ran a restaurant below on which, a confirmed Francophile, she bestowed a name reminiscent of a provincial French bistro — The Hungry Horse.

When Thurston vacated the upstairs area she suggested that it might serve as a gallery. Enter the rich and eccentric Major Harold de Vahl Rubin, a noted Queensland collector in search of an exhibition space in Sydney. He took it and employed Betty O'Neill to run it.

The opening of the Hungry Horse Gallery was a bizarre affair. Rubin sent out urgent reply-paid telegrams for an inaugural lunch at the restaurant below. These caused quite a stir as they were delivered to lawyers in court, doctors in the middle of operations. Three days before the scheduled opening Rubin despatched from his Brisbane home three armoured cars full of pictures. Not your average paintings these, but important works by Degas, Renoir, Monet. But O'Neill was given strict orders not to hang them, so they were stacked three or four deep on the floor.

At the appointed hour, guests arrived at the restaurant and were seated — eager collectors, artists, ladies and gentlemen of the press. They waited. And waited. Thurston had created a fine meal and fretted about the food being spoiled.

ABOVE: Sketch of The Hungry Horse
LEFT: Exterior of Lucio's Italian
Restaurant

Eventually the Major arrived, stood before his guests and, without saying a word, produced from his pocket an electric razor and began shaving. When finished, he bellowed to Thurston to bring on lunch. Immediately after eating, he departed.

In the ensuing month, thousands of people stormed through the new gallery. Queues formed along Elizabeth Street, much to the amusement of the regulars sinking their schooners at the Windsor Castle pub opposite. Thurston's gentleman friend was hired to guard the trove, but O'Neill was under orders neither to hang the pictures nor to sell any. After six months, O'Neill rang the Major to say that this was not the kind of gallery she had in mind. Besides, he had not paid her any wages. The armoured vans were immediately sent to collect the pictures, O'Neill received her cheque and so ended the first chapter in the story of this restaurant-cum-gallery.

Now at that time there was but one gallery in Paddington, Rudy Komon's, and O'Neill was egged on by various painter friends to open another. Thus did the famous Hungry Horse Gallery with (and please forgive the pun) its stable of twelve abstract artists come into being, inaugurating a long and felicitous conjunction of building, food, contemporary art and artists.

For her first exhibition, O'Neill chose a group of enormous canvases by Robert Hughes and the ever-unpredictable Rubin flew down from Queensland and bought the lot. He gave O'Neill a cheque for her commission and told her to send the pictures to him at the end of the show. She did so but, knowing Rubin a little better this time, instructed the pantechnicon driver not to hand over the pictures without payment. No payment was forthcoming so the pictures were returned, Rubin claiming that Hughes had killed one of his pet birds and buried it and this was his way of getting even. Hughes explained. He had been invited to Rubin's house to view the collection. As he wandered around he found himself in a large aviary where a dead bird lay on the ground. Thinking he was doing the right thing, he buried it, hence the Major's wild accusation of ornitholocide.

Excitement of one sort or another characterised the 1960s, especially the art world, even in places as remote from the twin centres of creative activity, New York and London, as Sydney. In 1963, twelve up-and-coming artists — Frank Hodgkinson, Stanislaus Rapotec, Charles Reddington, William Rose, Carl Plate, Colin Lanceley, John Olsen, Leonard Hessing, Robert Klippel, John Coburn, Robert Hughes and Emanuel Raft — posed on that lacework balcony of The Hungry Horse for what has become one of the defining photographs of Australian art history. Almost all went on to fame and, in some cases, fortune, a higher than average success rate in a chancy profession.

But the gallery was not to last. Never one to linger long in any restaurant, Thurston moved on. The place, upstairs and downstairs, was taken over by Ruth Schneider and Jackie Barbie, who made a great success of the restaurant, while Betty O'Neill moved on to join Kym Bonython in nearby Victoria Place.

BELOW: Bronze plaque awarded to Lucio's by the Italian Academy of Cuisine, 1997

BOTTOM: Restaurant interior

Schneider was a familiar Paddington figure, moving through its picturesque streets on a bicycle with a pannier in front, dressed as a latter-day Heidi with long blonde beribboned plaits and a gingham dirndl. With her departure and that of her partner, the restaurant was very briefly Bibi's and then, from 1983 (and for many more years to come, one hopes), consistently and triumphantly Lucio's, named for the new owner, Lucio Galletto, who moved here from Balmain via Natalino's, in its own time the most celebrated Italian restaurant in Sydney — as is Lucio's now. Thus began the glory days of this building as home to one of our most admired eating stations.

Sydney is a fickle town. It takes stamina and style to stay at the top of the heap for fifteen years and more, particularly in the restaurant business. This building started

its late twentieth-century life as a gallery plus restaurant and is, to some extent, still that today, although with the restaurant in the ascendancy and the art serving as a unique background for dining. Galletto has always collected art, always been kind to artists. The legacies of this mutual admiration are the handsome Blackmans, Storriers and Olsens decorating the dining rooms of his restaurant.

Restaurant is perhaps an inadequate word, for Lucio's is more a kind of salon, or at least the closest thing we have to one in Sydney. One goes there in the certain knowledge that the atmosphere will be warm, the company congenial, that there will be a number of agreeable people with whom to exchange pleasantries or ideas. Beyond its salonesque attributes is its status as an institution. Everyone knows Lucio's. Everyone loves Lucio's. The benign Lord McAlpine sets up headquarters here when he visits Sydney, doing three lunches and three dinners during a three-day visit. Why bother moving when it is so pleasant to be here?

Hither are drawn tycoons, the shakers and the shaken, budding plutocrats, fading stars. But most of all artists. Any good salon needs a peppering of creative types and they have always seemed attracted to this spot.

It is a happy place.

Leo Schofield

LEFT: Artists' lunch
(left to right) John Coburn,
Fred Cress, John Beard,
Tim Storrier, Garry Shead,
Lucio, Tom Lowenstein and
John Olsen

ABOVE TOP: Colin Lanceley and
Michael Johnson

ABOVE: Charles Blackman
and Lucio

Introduction

Lucio at the bar

OPPOSITE: John Olsen,
*How they made great chefs
in Italy*, 1995, pen on paper

I've known two Australian restaurateurs who were real friends to artists and writers. One was the late and sorely missed Georges Mora, who ran the Balzac in Melbourne in the 1960s. The other is Lucio Galletto, in Sydney, today. Italian food has always been my favourite, and of all the Italian restaurants I have eaten in over the last forty years, in Australia, America, England and Italy itself, Lucio's is very high on the list. In Australia it is right at the top. Mind you, I don't pretend to be unbiased. Its location means a lot to me too. That terrace house at 47 Windsor Street in Paddington is saturated in memories from the early 1960s, when the Australian art world was a lot smaller than it is now. It contained a gallery and a restaurant, both called The Hungry Horse. The gallery soon swallowed the restaurant, which was no great loss to gastronomy. Its stable — for once the demeaningly equine term for artists represented by a gallery seems to fit — was quite large, because the world of Sydney galleries was so small. It included Colin Lanceley and Bill Rose, Carl Plate and Stanislaus Rapotec, Frank Hodgkinson, Leonard Hessing, Charles Reddington, John Olsen, Robert Klippel, John Coburn, Emanuel Raft and, as a very junior colt, myself. One day its enterprising owner had the idea of publishing a calendar that reproduced the work of her artists. Never before, and never since, had I seen one of my own paintings printed in colour. This precious document included a group photo of the lot of us, perched insecurely on the narrow frilly balcony of no. 47, looking like a bunch of magpies on a telephone wire, a message from the days before artists (some of them, anyway) learned to arrange themselves in an easy-looking way for the camera. It now hangs on the wall of Lucio's restaurant, near the reception desk. Whenever I pass it I am seized, not by nostalgia exactly, but by a sense of irrecoverable *temps perdu*.

Was that long-haired creature with bat ears and a cigarette really me? What turned him into the ninety-five-kilo, sixty-year-old person now staring at his vanished and wiry self? Easy: it was fatal self-indulgence, abetted by people like Lucio, the master cooks, the entrepreneurs of Linguine alle Vongole and butter-drenched Cappesante alla Griglia and unctuous Risotto ai Funghi Porcini and seductive, crisply coated Costoletta di Vitello alla Milanese, their dark-blonde, breadcrumbed surfaces sprinkled with just enough raw chopped tomatoes and basil to make you think of them as health-food. Especially when washed down with a few glasses of Pinot Grigio and tamped, as it were, with a slice or two of Pecorino, less than thirty days old.

That floridly conservative English genius Evelyn Waugh used to hold that no country could be considered civilised if it had not been subjugated by Rome. In gastronomic terms, at least in the West and its cognate nations, this is largely true. Even the enormous superstructure of French cuisine was raised on Italian foundations, laid in the sixteenth century when Francois I imported his court cooks from Milan to relieve the meat-headed monotony of medieval Burgundian cooking, formal and heavy. The genius of Italian cuisine was to enshrine the fact that food should be the most natural thing in the world, made of fresh materials, locally grown, in which the principal ingredient of a dish was deferred to and enhanced by the *contorni*, or surroundings, not gussied up and rendered

unrecognisable by elaborate sauces. Italian food is essentially vernacular — not 'humble', not by any means, but very much part of the common speech of accessible pleasure. It has its pompous outgrowths, such as the tradition of *monsu* cuisine in the baroque South, developed to suit the banquet-tastes of the invading Bourbons, the colonising French. It has its vulgar colonial branches, such as the reliance on meatballs and burnt tomato sauce that used to permeate the Italian restaurants of downtown New York thirty years ago — 'home cooking' for transplanted Sicilians whose mothers were probably terrible cooks to begin with. But Italian food remains a living language with ancient roots that wind back to the village market and the *casa colonica*: it has various accents, Australian included. It has never ceased to grow and adapt, but its classic forms remain essentially the same — as they should, because they are the Truth. Food, and particularly Italian food, is a conservative art and is bound to be — though 'conservative' does not mean 'hidebound'. It refers to the conservation of tribal knowledge, a process slowly conducted under the eyes of the past with your own eyes and tastebuds open and alert. There has never been such a thing as an avant-garde in the art of Italian cooking, as there has been in painting or sculpture. The only attempt at it was made more than three-quarters of a century ago by the leader of the Futurists, Filippo Tommaso Marinetti, who proposed a *cucina futurista* whose ghastly and discordant dishes featured sauces of pistachio, chocolate, raw meat and eau-de-cologne. He even wanted to abolish pasta — 'It induces scepticism and pessimism. Spaghetti is no food for fighters.' But then, Marinetti was just another Fascist at heart, and I doubt if he would have got a table at Lucio's.

You learn to eat by cooking. You learn to cook by eating. It is an immemorial cycle, transmitted down the generations. My friend John Olsen, who eats at Lucio's all the time, gave him a drawing that exactly expresses this: it shows Lucio's imagined parents in a flurry of preparation in the kitchen, the table and the very air filled with a wild but purposeful tangle of movement and ingredients, while two small children — Lucio and Marino — stare in round-eyed fascination at the wonders that are going on, like infants who find themselves in an alchemist's study, absorbing everything not by precept but by example. Its caption is *How they made great chefs in Italy*.

ABOVE: Tim Storrier, Menu for Tim's party, 1993

OPPOSITE TOP: John Olsen, Pen drawing on menu, 1992

OPPOSITE BOTTOM: Robert Jacks, Pen drawing on menu, 1998

My childhood, in the 1940s and 1950s, wasn't like that. Not a bit. Food was still largely regarded by Australians as fuel: lumpy, charred and undistinguished — in sum, colonial English. 'Gourmet' food (that disastrous word) was a steak Diane, flamed in brandy to the imminent peril of your girlfriend's beehive. 'Italian' food, as I remember it, was rather watery ravioli served in a now long-defunct coffee shop called Lorenzini's. But then, things began to take off. This we owed to immigration. Foes of multiculturalism should remember what Australian food was like in the days of monoculture, and thank their Protestant gods for the change. *Mestizaje es grandeza*: mixture is greatness. 'A new dish,' wrote that garrulous eighteenth-century gourmet Anthelme de Brillat-Savarin, 'gives more pleasure to mankind than the discovery of a new star.' This is still true, and thirty-five years ago practically all dishes were new to Australians, so that they slid easily into a culture which, in other areas, was fiercely dedicated to the pleasures of the body. The evolution of Australian food into one of the great eclectic cuisines of the world parallels the astounding rise in quality and variety of Australian wines. All of this has happened — though its foundations were laid earlier, of course — in the years that I've been living out of Australia, so that every year, when I come back, I find myself surprised and enchanted all over again. Australia may first have been settled by hard men (and women too) but it was civilised by gentle, imaginative and skilled ones, people like Lucio Galletto. *Salute, e tanti auguri, Maestro*.

ROBERT HUGHES

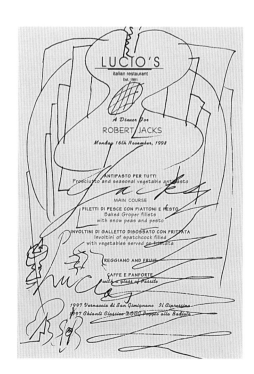

The Horse Bolted

To begin. First there was a restaurant and its name was The Hungry Horse, and when the horse grew up it became a famous art gallery as well. On a fragile cast-iron balcony of the art gallery, artists perilously perched and looked down on the sacred site which is the corner of Windsor and Elizabeth streets, Paddington. Suddenly the horse bolted and became the most famous restaurant of all, Lucio's Italian Restaurant.

Perhaps it didn't quite happen that way, but as the years winked by that's how it seemed to me.

The new owners were Lucio Galletto and Marino Maioli, fresh with new ideas about Italian food. On reflection it could be called *cucina sana*, but that sounds too fussy, for it seems to put a limitation on its intention. For it looked to quality and freshness of ingredients, where the ingredients maintain their individuality within the enormous vocabulary of Italian recipes, and the tradition remains secure.

There were freshly made pasta, large and different-shaped ravioli stuffed with crabs, prawns and spinach, in what seemed to be endless combinations, served with discrete and unctuous sauces.

Constant travellers have told me that Lucio's Tagliolini alla Granseola (green pasta with blue swimmer crab) is as good as, if not better than, any they have tasted in Italy.

There is a dish, it could be called a signature dish, for which freshness is so paramount that it must be ordered the day before. It is Pesce al Sale. Lucio uses snapper. Only Lucio serves this, presented whole and covered in a salt cast, at a table next to you. The silence and anticipation are religious. Lucio lifts the cast whole, and the aroma which arises from the concealed fish is something to dream about. Then the maestro slices the flaky but juicy fish into portions. Still all remains in silence. With an artist's sense of abstraction, Lucio judiciously drizzles the finest virgin olive oil over the portions, adding a squeeze of lemon juice, a pinch of parsley, a turn of black pepper and tiny chopped, seeded tomatoes.

Ecco — it is done! Spontaneously everyone claps; how's that for a one-man exhibition?

Simple? Not at all. When the salt emulsion that covers the fish is put into the oven it may not be touched or prodded. The salt cast must be mixed to the right consistency, else all will be disaster. The snapper must be removed at exactly the right moment.

From the beginning the restaurant was a success. Everyone intimated that something good was happening. For artists something special was at hand. Lucio and Marino loved art and artists (artists delight in being patted) and pictures were brought — some in lieu of dinners, some as simple gifts to a gifted and generous restaurateur.

This book is a salute to this modest but great restaurant that shares moments of happiness and will remain in the corner of our hearts.

JOHN OLSEN

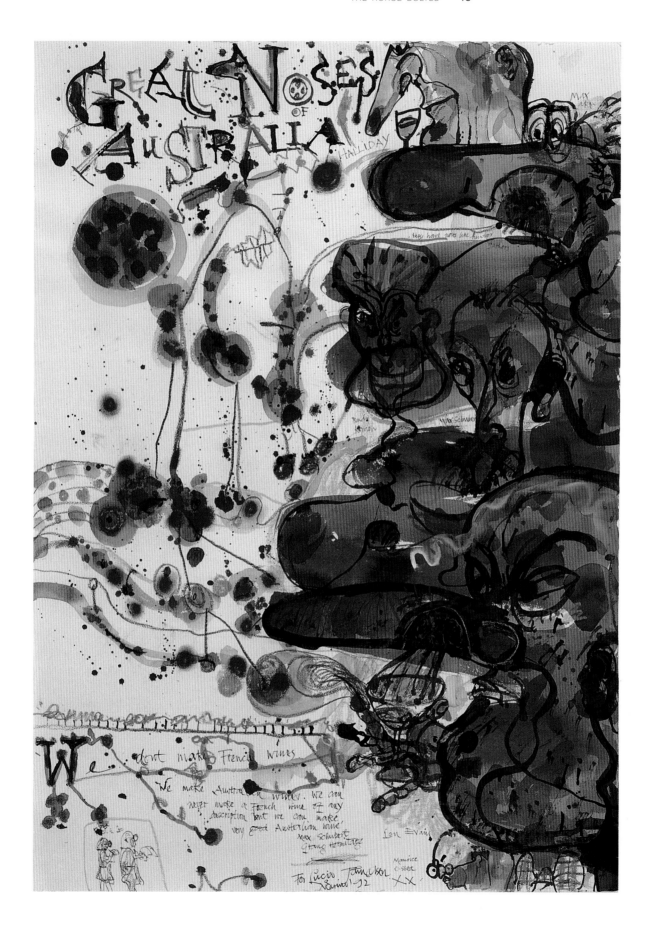

Lucio Galletto in conversation with David Dale

Bryan Westwood, *Portrait of Lucio*, 1997, oil on canvas

You started training to be an architect in Italy, and now you're running a restaurant in Australia. How did that come about?

I was almost born in a restaurant, actually. Back in 1950, before I was born, my family had started a restaurant — Capannina Ciccio at Bocca di Magra, on the coast where Liguria meets Tuscany. Coming back from school, we kids would go to the restaurant instead of home. We grew up between the tables and the stove.

But it's part of the peasant culture, I suppose, that parents always want their children to get a better education than they did. I was pushed by my family to study, so I started at technical college with a course that leads on to architecture, and I was working part-time at Ciccio.

Then when I was twenty-one, an Australian girl called Sally came to the restaurant to visit her sister, who was married to my cousin Mario. It was love at first sight. We married eighteen months later and we came to Australia. And of course I had to start a restaurant.

Do you ever think about what life might be like if you were an architect?

Now, I cannot imagine being an architect at all. All the time that I was with my family in Ciccio's, I didn't realise how much I loved the restaurant life. I would hear them saying, 'Look, I found this special basil, it gets the sun at the right time of day.' As a kid, I couldn't see why they were getting so excited about basil. Now I realise it was the beginning of my obsession never to compromise on quality.

All the kids used to complain about having to help in the restaurant. The river and the sea were at the end of our street, but if we wanted to go for a swim, first we had to cut up garlic and parsley with a *mezzaluna*. We'd say, 'Oh no, can't we go now?' Then after, we would go down to the beach with a knife and lemon and eat mussels.

When I started at college, I was thinking of my time in the restaurant as just a bit of work while I waited to do something else. My brother went to university, trained as a geologist, and he is now in the clothing business. He really regrets that. He loves food, he wishes he could do what I did. He says I am lucky, and I am.

Were your parents chefs?

My father was mainly in the dining room, while my mother was in the kitchen with my uncle Ciccio and Zia Anna (Mario's parents). It was a huge family and everybody worked there. The social life revolved around the restaurant. We never really went shopping. The fishermen would bring their catch to the restaurant, as would the onion seller and the tomato vendor. In fact all produce was locally grown, so everything served in the restaurant was seasonal. I used to go with my father up into the mountains to find the best olive oils. On the way we would stop at trattorias and osterias, to have a sandwich or a pasta.

LEFT: Andrew and Timothy

BELOW: Sidney Nolan, Drawing on docket slip, 1984

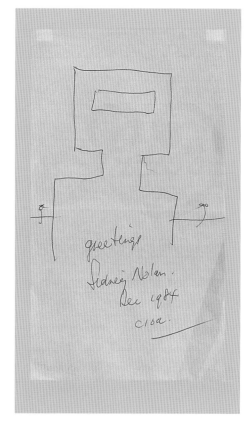

My uncle Ciccio was a very creative chef. He wasn't happy to do what the others were doing. He was always trying new things. He invented something called Tartina alla Ciccio, which is still today a specialty of the restaurant. It is a thick slice of bread soaked in fish broth, dipped in egg yolks then floured and lightly fried. Finally it is topped with prawns, calamari, scampi and other shellfish and a dollop of home-made mayonnaise.

Ciccio is also famous for the Zuppa di Datteri, which is made with the rare local sea dates, a kind of mussel found only in a ten-kilometre radius. The seafood antipasto selection is wonderful, and so is their famous Pesce al Sale, which is a whole fish baked under rock salt. That's a speciality we imported to Lucio's.

Did you ever do cooking yourself at Ciccio?

Never. I was spoiled. But I watched them, and when I started cooking, after I got married, it came naturally to me. But I've always preferred front of house. I like to know what's going on in the whole restaurant, not just the kitchen.

So what happened when you came to Australia with Sally?

That was in 1977. I couldn't speak much English, so naturally I looked for work in Italian restaurants. I started at Natalino's in Kings Cross. I worked hard for two years because I needed money and I needed to know what was happening in the food world of Australia. But most of the money I was earning was spent eating out with Sally. We hardly ate at home in those days. I really wanted to try all the restaurants in Sydney. The Sydney food scene was just starting to happen. We used to sit over dinner and say, 'If we had a restaurant, we should do it this way.'

What did you think of the Italian food you found in Sydney?

I was disappointed, actually. Coming from a restaurant like Ciccio, I found the Italian food in Sydney not very adventurous. They got stuck on scaloppine, which they would beat to death so there was no flavour left. They used cheap cheese, cheap ham, iceberg lettuce for salads. The place that really stood out was Beppi's. I have always respected Beppi because he had the highest standards even when a lot of the customers did not appreciate what he was doing.

Then in 1979, Pulcinella restaurant opened in Kings Cross. It shared a back lane with Natalino's. I met Armando Percuoco [who now runs Buon Ricordo restaurant in Paddington] and we used to have these long conversations about how French food was too dominant in Sydney and how one day Italian restaurants would beat the French. He was right. I think the Italians have won that battle now, but maybe not the war.

So when did you open your own place?

In 1981 I opened in Balmain, with financial help and support from my father-in-law and plenty of elbow-grease from our friends. We took over a restaurant called Gables, and we called it Lucio's because it was easy to pronounce and short enough to remember. I really liked Balmain because it felt like a village, and I grew up in a village.

We had a few problems in the beginning, because Sydney people were used to a different kind of Italian food — scaloppine and tomato paste and so on. We used to do different things, like Pesce al Cartoccio, a whole fish baked in silver foil with white wine, rosemary and garlic. We started to make our own fresh pasta, which nobody was doing at the time in Sydney. People were used to spaghetti and penne and we were doing home-made tagliatelle and fettuccine.

Then in 1983 a restaurant called Bibi's, on the site of the old Hungry Horse in Paddington, came on the market. I bought it with Marino Maioli, my partner until 1997. By the time we came to Paddington, attitudes had changed a little. We started with the home-made large ravioli, stuffed with ricotta and spinach, with a sauce of tomato and basil. That was our signature. And then the tagliolini, which we first did with small mussels, and later with crab. Our Tagliolini alla Granseola has appeared on every menu since.

Fred Cress, Menu, 1995

When we opened, my cousin Mario came to Australia and suggested we do the Gamberi e Fagioli, which is white cannellini beans and steamed prawns dressed with caviar and extra virgin olive oil. That was an instant success, both because of the interesting combination of flavours and because we were preparing it in the dining room. We also served whole fish filleted at the table.

I wanted to create the Italian feeling of service. In the beginning we couldn't deliver the service I wanted. That developed over time.

Were the dishes created by you?

Some were traditional Italian dishes adapted for a more modern and healthy way of eating. Others were worked out in collaboration with the chefs.

Victor Rubin, Pencil drawings on napkins, 1999

A chef called GeGe Riva arrived almost a year after we started, from London. He's a natural, who learned on the job. To work with him was exciting. We used to sit up till two o'clock in the morning talking about food and art.

After a while GeGe came up with his own ideas, which were wonderful. We started to see a nicer presentation, more northern Italian style, more refined. We used to read about Gualtiero Marchesi, who was reinventing Italian food at the time, and we felt more free to experiment than if we were in Italy. Both GeGe and I had the highest respect for the Italian tradition, but in a new country you have more room to move.

Over the years, with research and experimentation on flavours and colours, we created what you might call the Lucio's Style. The idea is to achieve a balance of taste and presentation, all done with love of nature and simplicity.

In 1996, when Timothy Fisher took over the kitchen, he brought with him a tremendous enthusiasm, along with professionalism and modesty. His skills mean we can continue to perfect the Lucio's Style.

How did the association with art come along?

Geoffrey Dutton, the poet, used to be a regular in the early days and he used to talk to me about The Hungry Horse, the restaurant and art gallery that was here in the 1960s, and the artists who used to eat here. No wonder I felt so comfortable when I first stepped in — the place had so much history of art and food.

Staff meal

Geoffrey brought in a photograph of a group of artists on the balcony. For me, these names were legends, heroes from a time I'd never known. Then one time Geoffrey came in with John Olsen, who liked the restaurant and brought in Tim Storrier — then Sidney Nolan, Donald Friend, Charles Blackman, and so it began.

All the works of art featured in the book are by artists who have been not only regular customers, but also good friends. The first time Sidney Nolan came in he did a little drawing of Ned Kelly on a piece of paper, which I spent a fortune to have framed. Next time he came in and saw it so well framed, he was impressed and did some others.

I know the artists understand that I take pride in having their work on display. I respect them tremendously. It gives me a lot of pleasure to have the art here. I work very hard, but with the art around me, it doesn't feel like work.

So now there's a book as well as a restaurant. Are you calling this a cookbook or an art book?

This book is about food, art and people. That is what Lucio's is about. I want the book to be the real thing: what the customers see when they come here. The substance will be there, in the recipes of what we have been cooking for fifteen years. But I decided I wanted it to be not just a recipe book. It has to be a visual book as well, because the restaurant is a visual experience.

So could we say that the book combines the architect's eye and the restaurateur's palate?

Well, possibly, but during my childhood there was art on the walls of my family's restaurant, collected from local artists. During the 1970s, Ciccio even had an art gallery connected to the restaurant. So you could just say once again that I am going back to my beginnings in Bocca di Magra.

Notes on Recipes

From all the recipes that we have presented over the years, we have selected, for this book, those that we feel most reflect our style and our philosophy towards food and serving it.

We have also tried to choose those recipes that can be made easily with everyday kitchen utensils and to write them in a way that makes them accessible to all who love good food but are not professional chefs with a brigade of assistants in tow.

With the exception of the pasta doughs and the desserts, all quantities are approximate — a little more or a little less of something will not ruin the end result.

We leave the seasoning to your taste, and cooking times are a guide only, as all ovens differ.

We hope that you will enjoy these recipes and use your creativity to make them your own.

Our greatest satisfaction will be to know that we have participated in making a gathering memorable.

LUCIO GALLETTO   TIMOTHY FISHER

Lucio with chef Timothy Fisher

bruschette e stuzzichini

ABOVE Cristobal serving Bellini

PAGE 22 John Coburn, *Study for Bruschetta*, 1998, watercolour

Lucio's restaurant was formerly The Hungry Horse, and in 1962 Betty O'Neill asked me to lunch there. She told me she was opening an art gallery above the restaurant to be called The Hungry Horse Gallery. I agreed to show with her, and her opening exhibition included works by John Olsen, Colin Lanceley, Robert Hughes, Charles Reddington, Frank Hodgkinson, Carl Plate, Robert Klippel, Emanuel Raft and myself. We were photographed together standing on the front balcony of the gallery and the photograph became an icon of Sydney art of the 1960s. A copy of it hangs in Lucio's restaurant along with works by many of the original Hungry Horse group, plus many by younger artists of the 1970s, 1980s and 1990s. Lucio's has become, since Lucio took over fifteen years ago, the artists' restaurant of Sydney.

JOHN COBURN

bruschetta
BASIC BRUSCHETTA

Any wood-fired or Italian bread loaf
Garlic cloves, peeled
Extra virgin olive oil

Slice the bread to about 1 cm thick. Toast on both sides. Rub one side with garlic and then brush with the olive oil.

NOTE If serving the bruschetta without topping, drizzle the olive oil instead of brushing.

bruschetta alla caprese
TOMATO AND BOCCONCINI BRUSCHETTA

2 fresh tomatoes, seeded and diced
1 fresh bocconcini of mozzarella, diced
4 fresh basil leaves, chopped
2 tblsp extra virgin olive oil
4 slices of Basic Bruschetta (see above)

In a bowl, mix all the ingredients together. Season and serve on bruschetta.
SERVES 4

bruschetta con puré di olive e pomodori essicati al sole
OLIVE PURÉE AND SUN-DRIED TOMATO BRUSCHETTA

4 slices of Basic Bruschetta (see above)
Olive purée
Sun-dried tomatoes
Fresh oregano, chopped

Spread the bruschetta with olive purée. Place julienned strips of sun-dried tomatoes on top and sprinkle with oregano.
SERVES 4

NOTE Olive purée, or tapenade, is available at delicatessens.

The orders

BRUSCHETTA (*CLOCKWISE*):
CON SARDINE MARINATE; ALLA CAPRESE;
DI PEPERONI ARROSTO E BOCCONCINI >

Jason Benjamin, *You are
never where you say you are*,
1997, oil on canvas

bruschetta con sardine marinate
MARINATED SARDINE BRUSCHETTA

3 cloves garlic, finely chopped
Fresh parsley, finely chopped
2 small chillies, roughly chopped
1 kg fresh sardine fillets
White wine vinegar (enough to cover)
Extra virgin olive oil (enough to cover)
6 slices of Basic Bruschetta (see page 26)

Combine the garlic, parsley and chilli. In a flat, high-sided dish, lay the sardines and sprinkle them with the garlic and parsley mixture. Cover them completely with the vinegar and leave them to rest for 5 days in the refrigerator.

Drain the sardines and pat dry slightly. Put them in another flat, high-sided dish, then cover them with the olive oil and let them rest for a further 2 days.

To serve, top bruschetta with the drained sardines.

SERVES 6

Fred Cress, Pen drawing
done at the table, 1991

bruschetta di peperoni arrosto e bocconcini
ROAST CAPSICUM AND BOCCONCINI BRUSCHETTA

4 slices of Basic Bruschetta (see page 26)
1 fresh bocconcini of mozzarella
2 Roast Capsicums (see page 34)
½ bunch fresh oregano, chopped
Extra virgin olive oil

Slice the bocconcini into thin discs. Cut the roast capsicums into strips, arrange them on the bruschetta and top with the bocconcini. Sprinkle with oregano and drizzle with olive oil.

SERVES 4

bruschetta di vongole e cozze
VONGOLE AND MUSSEL BRUSCHETTA

Salvatore Zofrea, *Study for Psalm 64*, pencil and watercolour

200 g vongole
300 g mussels
4 tblsp extra virgin olive oil
1 clove garlic, crushed
1 chilli, finely chopped
½ bunch fresh parsley, chopped
8 slices of Basic Bruschetta (see page 26)

Clean and wash the vongole and mussels thoroughly under running water to remove any sand. Heat a large frying pan, add the vongole and mussels and cook over high heat until they open (about 2–3 minutes). Discard any that do not open. Remove mussel and vongole meat from the shells and chop finely. Drain the shellfish, reserving 1 tablespoon of their liquid.

In another frying pan, heat the olive oil and garlic and cook over low heat until the garlic starts to turn golden brown. Remove and discard the garlic, then add the chilli, chopped shellfish and reserved liquid. Cook over high heat until the liquid evaporates.

Add parsley to the shellfish mixture and spread on the bruschetta.

SERVES 8

bruschetta di zucchine alla griglia e caprino
GRILLED ZUCCHINI AND GOAT'S CHEESE BRUSCHETTA

2 zucchini
180 g fresh goat's cheese
Extra virgin olive oil
6 slices of Basic Bruschetta (see page 26)

Cut the zucchini into long thin slices, brush with olive oil and grill briefly on high until lightly browned.

Top the bruschetta with the zucchini and goat's cheese and drizzle with olive oil.

SERVES 6

polenta e baccalà
GRILLED POLENTA WITH SALT COD

¼ salt cod (approximately 1200 g)
2 leeks
20 g butter
200 g mashed potatoes
100 ml pure cream
60 ml extra virgin olive oil
¼ quantity Polenta (see page 157)
Fresh chives, to serve

Soak the salt cod for 48 hours, changing the water 2–3 times a day. Poach the cod in simmering water for 8–10 minutes. Sweat leeks in butter for 10 minutes over low heat then purée until fine.

Flake the cod into the mashed potato. Add purée of leeks, the cream and olive oil. Grill slices of polenta, top with potato mixture and sprinkle with chopped chives.

SERVES 6

tartina di polenta con paté di fegatini
GRILLED POLENTA WITH DUCK LIVER PATÉ

Olive oil for frying
250 g duck livers, cleaned
1 onion, diced
2 cloves garlic, sliced
½ bunch fresh sage, chopped
250 ml good quality port
150 g butter, softened
¼ quantity Polenta (see page 157)

In a large frying pan, heat olive oil and cook duck livers for 3 minutes on each side over high heat. Place in a sieve to drain any extra blood that may come out.

In the same pan, sweat the onion and garlic for 5 minutes over low heat. Add sage and port and simmer until liquid is reduced by half.

In a blender, process duck livers and onion mixture until fine. Add butter and mix well.

Grill strips of polenta until golden brown and spread paté on top. Serve immediately.

SERVES 6

George Raftopoulos, Ceramic plate, 1998

Garry Shead, *Le Déjeuner sur l'herbe*, 1992, oil on canvas

olive liguri in marinata classica
LIGURIAN OLIVES IN CLASSIC MARINADE

Ligurian olives
Fennel seeds
Orange zest
Lemon juice
Garlic cloves, peeled
Extra virgin olive oil (enough to cover the olives)

Rinse the olives under running water and pat dry with a paper towel.

Mix all ingredients in a large bowl and allow to stand for at least 12 hours in the refrigerator.

To serve, remove the garlic and the orange zest and drain off the liquid.

NOTE We have left the quantities in this recipe to personal taste. Ligurian olives will keep for up to 1 week if covered and refrigerated.

olive nere con finocchio e basilico
KALAMATA OLIVES WITH FENNEL AND BASIL

250 g Kalamata olives, pitted
1 fennel bulb
3 cloves garlic, peeled and bruised slightly using the back of a knife
5 fresh basil leaves, chopped
Extra virgin olive oil

Rinse the olives under running water and dry them in a salad spinner to remove all traces of water. Wash the fennel and cut it into pieces twice the size of the olives.

In a large bowl, combine the olives, fennel, garlic and basil. Drizzle with olive oil and mix until all ingredients are well combined. Remove the garlic before serving.

SERVES 6

olive nere con sedano, origano e peperoncino
KALAMATA OLIVES WITH CELERY HEARTS, OREGANO AND CHILLI

250 g Kalamata olives, pitted
4 celery hearts, diced
2 cloves garlic, peeled and bruised slightly using the back of a knife
Fresh oregano leaves, chopped very finely
1 chilli, very finely chopped
Extra virgin olive oil

Rinse the olives under running water and dry them in a salad spinner to remove all traces of water.

In a large bowl, combine the olives, celery, garlic, oregano and chilli. Mix well. Drizzle with the olive oil and mix until all ingredients are well combined. Remove the garlic before serving.

SERVES 6

John Coburn, Ceramic plate, 1998

peperoni arrosto
ROAST CAPSICUMS

6 red or yellow capsicums
3 tblsp extra virgin olive oil
Mixed herbs (optional)

Brush the capsicums with olive oil, place on a tray in a moderate oven and roast for about 20 minutes, turning them from time to time. Put capsicums in a plastic bag for a few minutes, so skin will come off more easily. Peel, seed and slice.

Add the remaining olive oil and chopped mixed herbs, if desired.

NOTE The capsicums can be used in some salads, as a topping on bruschetta, to complement main courses or as an ingredient in some pastas.

OLIVE NERE CON SEDANO,
ORIGANO E PEPERONCINO >

antipasti

The Space Between

It has been said that the painter Pierre Bonnard sought first and foremost to paint the savour of things, to recover their savour.

Looking does not necessarily mean seeing (as eating and drinking do not necessarily mean tasting). To see something is to explore it visually. Prolonged looking leads to seeing more, understanding and enjoying more — what Bonnard spoke of as 'the pleasure of seeing and its rewards'. It is an act of intelligent seeing.

Lucio's is an intelligent restaurant, perfectly blending feeling, thought and action. It is about a confirmation of structure and purpose that has evolved from experience and an understanding of the past. Tradition and skills are re-enacted here and magically fused with new ideas (respectfully muted when appropriate) to give definition to our own contemporary palate. It is not about a search for novelty, but about an elevation of spirit and conscience which we can discern by the manner in which an idea is realised and presented before us.

I am reminded of a definition of research by Chambers, the eighteenth-century composer–musicologist: 'Research, in music, is a kind of prelude or voluntary wherein the composer seems to search or look out for the strains or touches of harmony which he is to use in the regular piece to be played afterwards.' This seems appropriate to the working sensibilities that emanate from Lucio's kitchen, where what is created and prepared serves to educate as well as to delight us. The experience cultivates a greater awareness of sensory wonder and stimulates our receptivity towards aesthetic well-being. We leave the restaurant fulfilled in a complete sense rather than full in a sense that is basic.

The intervals or spaces between our active tasting and consumption are the intervals that establish the condition for a contemplative reflection on what we have experienced, or how the ordinary became extraordinary. Away from the restaurant we recall from memory our sensual inscriptions. It is the space between all things as well as the things themselves. It is what Mondrian meant when he said his goal was to undermine the distinction between foreground and background in painting. He wanted, he said, 'to give painting a holistic object-like quality all of its own'.

Returning to Lucio's is an act of confirmation — a means of rediscovery rather than an act of repetition. It cultivates the pleasure of discernment, a means by which we are able to measure and compare. It is somewhat akin to looking at Bonnard, or listening to Monteverdi, or reading Rilke — you have to do it often, a process that synthesises our knowing. It is the 'blood remembering' within us that creates a state of delicious anticipation for the next encounter.

JOHN BEARD

bresaola con insalata di sedano e parmigiano
BRESAOLA WITH CELERY HEART AND PARMESAN SALAD

Massimo Giannoni, Pencil
drawing, 1994

1 bunch celery (heart only)
90 g (1 cup) parmesan cheese, shaved
90 ml extra virgin olive oil
Salt and pepper to taste
48 slices bresaola

Wash and dry celery, cut very finely across the stick, and place in a bowl with the shaved parmesan and a little of the olive oil. Sprinkle with a little salt, if desired, and pepper.

Arrange an equal number of slices of bresaola on each serving plate. Place celery in the centre and drizzle the rest of the olive oil around the bresaola before serving.

SERVES 4

NOTE Bresaola is available from selected butchers and delicatessens.

cappesante e zucchine gialle
GRILLED SEA-SCALLOP MEAT WITH YELLOW SQUASH AND TOMATO COULIS

6 large vine-ripened tomatoes
100 ml extra virgin olive oil
Salt and pepper to taste
12 small yellow squash
1 kg extra large sea-scallop meat

Blanch tomatoes in boiling water for 1 minute and remove. Peel and seed the tomatoes. Place tomatoes in a blender and process for 3–4 minutes. Transfer the tomato purée to a medium saucepan with salt, pepper and 60 ml of the olive oil. Cook over low heat for 3 minutes.

Slice yellow squash about 3 mm thick. Boil squash in salted water for 2 minutes, drain and arrange in the centre of serving plates.

Under a hot grill, or in a hot frying pan, heat the remaining olive oil and cook the scallop meat for 1 minute on each side. Place the scallops on the yellow squash and pour the tomato coulis around.

SERVES 6

CAPPESANTE E ZUCCHINE GIALLE >

CARPACCIO ALLA MELAGRANA

carpaccio alla melagrana
BEEF CARPACCIO WITH POMEGRANATE

600 g beef fillet
1 pomegranate
Juice of 1 lime
50 ml extra virgin olive oil
1 punnet baby rocket

Remove any silver skin from the beef fillet, wrap the beef in cling film and freeze for about 30 minutes. Slice the beef very finely and divide the slices between 6 serving plates.

To make the pomegranate dressing, cut the pomegranate in half across the fruit. Using a teaspoon, remove the seeds, leaving the pith behind. Place pomegranate seeds, lime juice and olive oil in a bowl and mix well.

Wash and dry the rocket. Dress with a little of the pomegranate dressing and arrange a pile of rocket in the centre of each plate. Drizzle the remaining pomegranate dressing over the beef and serve immediately.

SERVES 6

carpaccio con trito di noci e radicchio
BEEF CARPACCIO WITH CHOPPED WALNUTS, CHIVES AND RADICCHIO

600 g beef fillet
240 g (2 cups) walnut pieces
6 leaves red radicchio
½ bunch chives, finely chopped
120 ml Lemon Juice Olive Oil (see page 156)

Remove any silver skin from the beef fillet, wrap in cling film and freeze for about 30 minutes. Slice the beef very finely and divide the slices between 6 serving plates.

Place walnuts on a baking tray and roast for 10 minutes at 180°C. Place the hot nuts into a teatowel and rub to remove the skins from the nuts. Allow to cool.

While the nuts are cooling, wash and dry the radicchio, then cut it very finely. When the nuts are cold, chop them and mix them with the radicchio, chives, and 90 ml of the lemon juice olive oil. Place the salad on top of the beef and drizzle the rest of the oil around.

SERVES 6

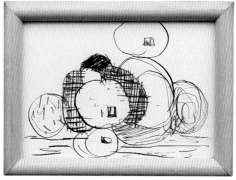

ABOVE: Chris Antico, Ink drawings, 1990

carpaccio di salmone marinato e asparagi
CARPACCIO OF SALT-CURED SALMON WITH ASPARAGUS

600 g Tasmanian salmon fillet
600 g (2 cups) rock salt
100 g (⅓ cup) white sugar
2 cloves garlic, peeled and crushed
2 bunches asparagus, trimmed
60 ml extra virgin olive oil

Remove any bones from the salmon, but leave the skin on the fish as this makes it easier to slice.

In a large bowl, combine the rock salt, sugar and crushed garlic. Place some of the salt mixture into a high-sided stainless steel, plastic or glass tray, add the salmon and cover with the remaining salt mixture. Cover the tray with cling film and refrigerate for 48 hours, turning the salmon once.

Remove the salmon from the tray, wash off any remaining salt, pat dry and slice very finely. Boil the asparagus for 3 minutes in salted water. Drain, place on a platter and drizzle the olive oil over the asparagus. Cover the asparagus stalks with the salmon.

SERVES 6

NOTE When you are marinating the salmon, use a high-sided stainless steel, plastic or glass tray because the salt draws the moisture out of the salmon. Do not use an aluminium tray as the metal will react with the salt.

David >

fegatini d'anatra con frittata e aceto balsamico
PAN-FRIED DUCK LIVERS WITH FRITTATA AND BALSAMIC VINEGAR

Walter

6 eggs
100 ml pure cream
½ bunch fresh thyme leaves, chopped
5 tblsp (⅓ cup) parmesan cheese, grated
1 onion, finely chopped
100 g butter
12 duck livers (large)
Extra virgin olive oil
Balsamic vinegar

Pre-heat oven to 180°C.

In a large bowl, place eggs, cream, thyme and parmesan. In a small, ovenproof frying pan, melt 50 g of the butter over medium heat. Add the onion and sweat until transparent. Pour the egg mixture into the frying pan and bake for 20 minutes at 180°C. Once cooked, allow the frittata to rest for 5 minutes, then cut it into slices.

In a large frying pan, melt the remaining butter and pan-fry the duck livers over high heat for 2 minutes on each side. Remove livers and allow to rest for 5 minutes.

Serve livers with slices of frittata and a splash of olive oil and vinegar.

SERVES 6

fegatini di pollo e verdure
GRILLED CHICKEN LIVERS WITH RATATOUILLE

John Olsen, *Portrait of Walter*,
1999, pen on paper

1 onion, peeled
1 red capsicum, seeded
1 yellow capsicum, seeded
1 stick celery
80 ml olive oil
2 zucchini, diced
200 ml Tomato Sauce (see page 158)
½ bunch fresh parsley, chopped
18 chicken livers
20 ml vegetable oil

Dice all vegetables the same size. In a large frying pan, heat the olive oil over low heat and sweat onion, capsicums and celery for 10 minutes. Add zucchini, tomato sauce and parsley. Cook for a further 5 minutes.

Baste chicken livers with vegetable oil and grill on high for 2 minutes on each side. When cooked, allow to rest in a warm place for 5 minutes.

To serve, divide the ratatouille among 6 serving plates and arrange the livers on top.

SERVES 6

fichi grigliati con endivia e funghi
MARINATED GRILLED FIGS WITH WITLOF AND SHIITAKE MUSHROOMS

John Olsen, Nude drawing,
1991, charcoal on paper

50 g (⅓ cup) brown sugar
90 ml red wine vinegar
300 ml olive oil
2 cloves garlic, sliced
1 bunch fresh tarragon, chopped
1 bunch fresh chervil, chopped
12 ripe figs
18 shiitake mushrooms
3 witlof
6 slices of Basic Bruschetta (see page 26)

In a large bowl, combine sugar and vinegar and leave for 5 minutes, or until sugar has dissolved. Add oil, garlic and herbs and whisk gently. Slice figs in half lengthways, place in marinade mix and allow to stand for 2 hours.

Cut witlof into long thin strips and shiitake mushrooms into halves. Cook mushrooms and figs under a hot grill, or in a very hot heavy pan until they are a nice nut-brown colour, then add them to the witlof. Place mushrooms and witlof on the slices of bruschetta with figs surrounding.

SERVES 6

fiori di zucchini ripieni
STUFFED ZUCCHINI FLOWERS WITH ASPARAGUS AND PARMESAN

2 bunches English spinach, cleaned
500 g ricotta cheese
100 g parmesan cheese, grated
2 egg yolks
20 zucchini flowers
120 ml extra virgin olive oil
2 bunches fresh asparagus, trimmed
80g Reggiano parmesan cheese, shaved

In a large pot of boiling water, blanch the spinach. Drain spinach and cut into fine strips, then mix with ricotta, grated parmesan and egg yolks. Open the zucchini flowers, cut out and discard the stigma, and fill the flowers with the ricotta mixture. Place zucchini flowers on a baking tray with 60 ml of the olive oil and bake for 15 minutes at 180°C.

Boil the asparagus in salted water for 3 minutes or until it is still a little firm to the touch. Shave the Reggiano parmesan with a vegetable peeler and combine with the remaining olive oil and the asparagus. Arrange the asparagus on four plates, with the tips facing out, and place the zucchini flowers in the centre.

SERVES 4

FIORI DI ZUCCHINI RIPIENI >

gamberi e carciofi
STEAMED PRAWNS WITH RAW ARTICHOKES AND PARMESAN CHEESE

2 kg green king prawns, shelled
6 globe artichokes
Juice of 3–4 lemons (120 ml)
Extra virgin olive oil
60 g Reggiano parmesan cheese, shaved

Steam king prawns for 5 minutes. Peel and discard the outer leaves of the globe artichokes. Slice the artichoke heart very, very thinly then mix with the lemon juice, olive oil and parmesan. Divide artichoke mixture among 6 serving plates. Top with prawns and a drizzle of olive oil.

SERVES 6

Frank Hodgkinson, Menu,
pen on paper

gamberi e fagioli
STEAMED PRAWNS WITH CANNELLINI BEANS AND SEVRUGA CAVIAR

375 g dried cannellini beans
1 head garlic, cut in half
1 onion, peeled and chopped
4 bay leaves
2 kg green prawns
80 ml extra virgin olive oil
6 tsp Sevruga caviar

Soak the cannellini beans in cold water for 10–12 hours before cooking. Drain beans and discard the soaking water.

In a medium pot, place beans, garlic, onion, bay leaves and enough water to cover. Bring to the boil, then reduce heat and simmer for 30 minutes. When cooked, remove beans from water and discard other ingredients.

Shell and devein prawns and steam for 5 minutes. In a large bowl, combine prawns, beans, olive oil and caviar and mix well. Serve immediately, dividing the beans among 6 serving plates and topping with the prawns.

SERVES 6

< GAMBERI E FAGIOLI

lingua di bue con puré di ceci e salsa al basilico
GRILLED OX TONGUE WITH CHICKPEA PURÉE AND BASIL DRESSING

200 g (1 cup) dried chickpeas
12 cloves garlic, peeled
1 large ox tongue (600 g)
1 carrot, peeled and chopped
1 stick celery, chopped
1 onion, peeled and chopped
2 bay leaves
80 ml extra virgin olive oil
Additional olive oil for grilling
Salt and pepper to taste
120 ml Basil Dressing (see page 156)

Soak chickpeas in cold water for 12 hours before cooking. Drain chickpeas and discard soaking water.

Place the chickpeas and 10 of the garlic cloves in a pot and cover with water. Cook on medium heat for 1½ hours or until chickpeas are tender. Once cooked, set aside.

Place tongue, carrot, celery, onion, bay leaves and the remaining garlic in a pot and cover with water. Bring to the boil, reduce heat and simmer for 1–1½ hours or until the tongue is tender and the skin peels off easily. Discard onion, carrot, celery and bay leaves. Peel tongue and cut it into 18 even slices. Drain chickpeas, retaining the cooked garlic cloves. In a blender, combine chickpeas, cooked garlic, olive oil, salt and pepper and purée until smooth.

Brush tongue slices with a little olive oil and grill on high for 3 minutes on each side.

To serve, place chickpea purée in centre of each serving plate, top with 3 slices of grilled tongue and drizzle basil dressing around.

SERVES 6

ostriche e trota cruda

PACIFIC OYSTERS WITH RAINBOW TROUT TARTARE AND FISH ROE

OSTRICHE E TROTA CRUDA

2 rainbow trout, filleted
½ bunch fresh chives, finely chopped
6 tsp fish roe
30 ml extra virgin olive oil
3 dozen Pacific oysters, shucked
Lemon wedges, to serve

Skin and dice the trout and combine with chives, fish roe and olive oil. Top oysters with tartare and serve with lemon wedges.

SERVES 6

< Garry Shead, Ceramic plate, 1998

polipetti alla griglia con finocchio e balsamico
GRILLED BABY OCTOPUS WITH FENNEL AND BALSAMIC VINEGAR

2 kg baby octopus (or 1200 g, cleaned)
40 ml vegetable oil
2 tblsp balsamic vinegar
6 tblsp extra virgin olive oil
3 heads fennel, cleaned and very finely sliced

Using a sharp knife, remove the heads and beaks from the octopus. Brush with vegetable oil and grill on high for 4–5 minutes. In a large bowl, combine octopus, balsamic vinegar, olive oil and fennel. Serve immediately.

SERVES 6

polipetti brasati alla salsa piccante
BRAISED OCTOPUS WITH TOMATO, CHILLI AND BLACK OLIVES

50 g unsalted butter
2 onions, finely diced
2 chillies, chopped
2 kg baby octopus (or 1200 g, cleaned)

1 500-g tin tomatoes
¼ cup black olives
½ bunch fresh basil leaves

Using a sharp knife, remove the head and beak from the octopus. In a large pot, heat butter over low heat and sweat onions and chillies for 10 minutes. Add cleaned octopus and crushed tomatoes. Bring to the boil, reduce heat and simmer for 1 hour or until octopus is tender. Add olives and basil just before serving.

SERVES 6

salmone con funghi, parmigiano e cuori di sedano
POACHED SALMON WITH CELERY HEARTS, MUSHROOMS AND PARMESAN CHEESE

1 carrot, peeled and chopped
1 onion, peeled and chopped
½ bunch fresh thyme
6 cloves garlic
600 g salmon fillets
Salt and pepper to taste

6 button mushrooms
4 sticks of celery hearts (use inner stalks only)
60 g Reggiano parmesan cheese, shaved
3 tblsp extra virgin olive oil

For poaching liquid, combine carrot, onion, thyme and garlic in a medium pot and add enough water to cover. Bring to the boil, then reduce heat and simmer for 10 minutes.

Cut salmon into 6 even pieces, season with salt and pepper and poach in cooking liquid for 4–5 minutes. The salmon should be pink in the middle. When cooked, remove with a slotted spoon.

Finely slice the button mushrooms and celery hearts, then combine with the parmesan and olive oil. Arrange on serving plates and top with salmon.

SERVES 6

< Chris Antico, *Picking Lemons*, 1997, oil on canvas

sardine in padella con pomodoro fresco
PAN-FRIED SARDINE FILLETS WITH DICED TOMATO, CAPERS AND PARSLEY

12 new potatoes
200 ml olive oil
800 g sardine fillets
100 g (¾ cup) cornflour
6 ripe tomatoes
½ bunch continental parsley, chopped
4 tblsp capers, washed
40 ml extra virgin olive oil, additional

Cut potatoes into 1-cm thick slices. Heat half of the olive oil over medium heat. Add potatoes and pan-fry until cooked (about 10 minutes). Remove from oil and drain on paper towel.

Trim any small fins off the sardine fillets. Coat fillets with cornflour, shaking off any excess. Heat the remaining olive oil over medium heat and pan-fry the sardines for 2 minutes on each side.

Peel and dice the tomatoes and combine with the parsley, capers and additional olive oil.

To serve, place fried potatoes on 4 plates and top with sardines. Arrange diced tomato mixture around the sardines.

SERVES 4

seppioline con radicchio rosso e capperi
MARINATED CUTTLEFISH WITH RADICCHIO AND CAPERS

1 carrot, peeled and chopped
1 onion, peeled and chopped
½ bunch thyme
8 cloves garlic, peeled
160 ml white wine vinegar
1½ litres water
2½ kg cuttlefish (or 1800 g, cleaned)
Juice of 1 lemon
Pinch cumin powder
300 ml extra virgin olive oil
2 heads red-leaf radicchio
100 g capers, washed

For poaching liquid, combine carrot, onion, thyme, 6 of the garlic cloves, vinegar and water in a pot. Bring to the boil, then reduce heat and simmer for 10 minutes.

Clean cuttlefish and poach in cooking liquid for 2–3 minutes. When cooked, remove cuttlefish and cut into fine strips. In a large bowl, combine cuttlefish, lemon juice, cumin and 200 ml of the olive oil.

Wash radicchio and discard the outer leaves. Finely slice the radicchio hearts, dress with the remaining olive oil, and add the capers. Arrange radicchio on serving plates and top with cuttlefish.

SERVES 6

NOTE To clean cuttlefish, remove the large beak, skin and insides. Wash under running cold water and pat dry with a paper towel.

Margaret Woodward,
Matisse and his Birds, 1995,
mixed media

Victor Rubin, *From the North West Corner*,
1995, oil on canvas >

tartara di pesce
SALMON TARTARE WITH SEVRUGA CAVIAR

480 g fresh salmon fillets
½ bunch chives, finely chopped
60 ml Lemon Juice Olive Oil (see page 156)
6 tsp Sevruga caviar
6 slices ciabatta bread

Remove any bones from the fish and cut into ½-cm dice with a sharp knife. In a large bowl, combine fish, chives and lemon juice olive oil. Divide among 6 serving plates and top with caviar. Serve immediately with slices of bread that have been baked in the oven for 4 minutes at 200°C.

To serve, place tartare in the middle of 6 plates with the bread on the side.

SERVES 6

NOTE This dish can also be made with tuna or kingfish.

terrina di verdure e caprino al pesto
ROAST VEGETABLE AND GOAT'S CHEESE TERRINE

John Coburn, *Portrait of Senbergs*, 1991, pen on paper done at the table

2 eggplants, sliced 1 cm thick
4 tblsp salt
4 zucchini, sliced 1 cm thick
60 ml extra virgin olive oil
150 g goat's cheese
80 ml cream
2 yellow Roast Capsicums (see page 34)
2 red Roast Capsicums (see page 34)

Place eggplant slices in colander, sprinkle with salt and allow to stand for 20 minutes to extract bitter juices. Wash and pat dry.

Place sliced eggplant and zucchini on a baking tray, sprinkle with olive oil and cook for 10 minutes in a moderate oven.

In a large bowl, mix the goat's cheese and cream until smooth. In a 20-cm terrine mould, layer all ingredients, starting with yellow capsicum, then eggplant, goat's cheese, red capsicum and zucchini. Repeat the process until all the ingredients are used up. Cover the terrine mould with cling film and place two 1-ltr milk cartons on top to press all the ingredients together. Allow to stand in the fridge for 2–4 hours, then turn out the terrine on a board and slice.

SERVES 6

George Raftopoulos, *Untitled*,
1998, oil on canvas

tonno, polenta e condimento
GRILLED YELLOW-FIN TUNA, GRILLED POLENTA AND CONDIMENT

600 g yellow-fin tuna
6 tsp ground fennel seeds
180 g (1¼ cup) Polenta (see page 157)
60 ml olive oil
180 g Mixed Capsicum and Red Wine Vinegar Condiment (see page 150)

Cut tuna into 6 even slices and sprinkle with ground fennel seeds. Cut polenta into
desired shapes and grill on high for 1 minute on each side. Place polenta on a tray and
leave in a warm spot. Brush the tuna slices with olive oil and grill on high for 1 minute
on each side, keeping the tuna very rare so that it does not become dry. Arrange tuna
and polenta on 6 serving plates and spoon the condiment over.

SERVES 6

tortino di caprino e peperoni
TARTLET OF GOAT'S CHEESE, ROAST CAPSICUM AND CARAMELISED ONIONS

< TORTINO DI CAPRINO E PEPERONI

4 large onions, peeled and sliced
60 ml olive oil
160 g Short Savoury Pastry (see page 164)

2 red Roast Capsicums (see page 34)
160 g Kryton goat's cheese, sliced
12 fresh basil leaves, finely sliced
Extra virgin olive oil for drizzling

Place onions and olive oil in a large pot and cook over low heat for 2 hours, stirring from time to time. The onions should be a caramel colour (but not burnt).

Roll the savoury pastry into 4 individual tartlet moulds (approximately 5 cm in diameter) and allow to rest in the refrigerator for 15 minutes. Prick pastry with a fork and bake for 10 minutes at 180°C.

Divide onions among pastry cases, add a layer of capsicum then one of goat's cheese. Top with basil and drizzle with olive oil.

SERVES 4

NOTE If Kryton goat's cheese is unavailable, any good quality mild, creamy goat's cheese will do.

tortino di trippa e fagioli
TARTLET OF HONEYCOMB TRIPE AND HARICOT BEANS

160 g Short Savoury Pastry (see page 164)
40 ml olive oil
2 onions, peeled and finely diced
2 cloves garlic, crushed
400 g honeycomb tripe

200 ml Tomato Sauce (see page 158)
200 ml White Chicken Stock (see page 153)
200 g haricot beans (see method below)
50 g parmesan cheese, grated

Roll the savoury pastry into 4 individual tartlet moulds (approximately 5 cm in diameter) and allow to rest in the refrigerator for 15 minutes. Prick pastry with a fork and bake for 10 minutes at 180°C.

In a medium pot, heat olive oil. Add diced onions and garlic and cook over low heat for 10 minutes.

Cut tripe into small strips and add to the pot, stirring for 2 minutes. Add tomato sauce and chicken stock, reduce heat and simmer until the tripe is tender enough to cut with a fork (about 1½ hours). Add cooked beans, parmesan and butter and stir for 2–3 minutes. Serve in pastry cases.

TO COOK HARICOT BEANS

200 g (1 cup) dried haricot beans
2 cloves garlic, peeled
1 onion, peeled and chopped

1 stick celery
4 bay leaves

Soak haricot beans for 6–8 hours in cold water. Before cooking, drain beans and discard the soaking water. In a medium pot, combine beans, garlic, vegetables and bay leaves. Cover with water and simmer for 40 minutes or until beans are soft.

SERVES 4

Salvatore Zofrea, Ceramic plate, 1998

triglie in marinata di zafferano
SAFFRON-MARINATED RED MULLET

1½ kg red mullet
500 ml extra virgin olive oil
3 onions, peeled and finely sliced
200 ml white wine vinegar
3 pinches saffron threads
80 g (¾ cup) plain flour

Scale and fillet the mullet and remove any bones.

In a large saucepan, heat 100 ml of the olive oil, add the onions and cook over medium heat until tender (about 10 minutes). When the onions are cooked, add the vinegar and saffron, then set aside to let the saffron flavour infuse.

Coat the red mullet in the flour, shaking off any excess. In a frying pan, heat the remaining oil over medium heat and pan-fry the mullet for about 1 minute on each side. Layer the red mullet and the marinade in a serving dish and leave to marinate for 1 hour before serving.

SERVES 6

trota salmonata al pesto con patate e fagiolini
POACHED OCEAN TROUT WITH POTATOES, GREEN BEANS AND QUAIL EGGS

Charles Blackman,
Sketchbook drawing in
Venice, 1983

1 carrot, peeled and chopped
1 onion, peeled and chopped
½ bunch fresh thyme
6 cloves garlic
600 g ocean trout, filleted
Salt and pepper to taste
12 new potatoes
120 g green beans
9 quail eggs
3 tblsp extra virgin olive oil
½ quantity of Pesto (see page 156)

For poaching liquid, place carrot, onion, thyme and garlic in a medium pot and cover with water. Bring to the boil, then reduce heat and simmer for 10 minutes.

Cut ocean trout into 6 even pieces, season with salt and pepper and poach in cooking liquid for 4–5 minutes. The trout should be pink in the middle.

Wash the potatoes then boil them until a knife can cut them without any pressure.

Top and tail the beans and blanch in salted water.

In a small pot, cover the quail eggs with cold water, bring to the boil, reduce heat and simmer for 2½ minutes. Shell eggs and slice in half.

Slice the potatoes thinly and combine with the beans and olive oil.

To assemble, place beans and potatoes on serving plates, top with the trout and drizzle the pesto over.

SERVES 6

minestre

(PASTE, RISOTTI, ZUPPE)

What makes a restaurant Great, as opposed to merely good?

Here are some possible answers: a menu that changes seasonally, but not so much that the joy of surprise outweighs the security of old favourites. Cooking that is both adventurous and confident, founded on well-tried traditions and able to educate you into new sensations without making you feel like a guinea pig in an unfinished experiment. Service which anticipates the needs of diners and is ever watchful, adjusting its speed and its chattiness for each individual. A distance between tables that allows every diner to feel simultaneously private and part of a buzzing scene. Visual surroundings striking enough to be a topic of conversation if there's a lull at the table. A pricing policy which leaves every diner content that there's been value for money.

All of these details are essential to greatness, but they are not enough. Over-arching them all is one quality: generosity. The characteristic that unites all restaurants that have been called Great is a restaurateur who finds happiness in making others happy. When the pleasure of the customer is the pleasure of the restaurateur, all the other details fall naturally into place.

The quality of generosity seems to reside more in Italian restaurateurs than in those of any other nation. And Australia is the luckiest of countries because so many Italian chefs and waiters have brought their generosity to us.

The supreme example is Lucio's.

DAVID DALE

pasta nera
FRESH BLACK PASTA DOUGH

500 g (4 cups) plain flour
25 g cooking salt
1 whole egg

3 egg yolks
1 tblsp squid ink (available from good
    fish suppliers)

black pasta

TO PREPARE THE DOUGH On a clean workbench, mix flour and salt together and make a well in the centre. In a bowl, whisk egg, yolks and squid ink together. Pour mixture into the well in the flour and gradually mix in the flour with your hands until a dough forms. Knead for about 10 minutes, cover with cling film and allow to rest in the refrigerator for at least 30 minutes before using.

USING THE PASTA MACHINE Divide the dough into five balls. Flatten each ball with the palm of your hand until thin enough to fit between the rollers (approximately 1 cm).

Feed the dough through a pasta machine on the widest setting. Sprinkle the resulting strip with flour on both sides and fold into thirds. Repeat this feeding, flouring and folding 8 to 10 times, until the dough is smooth and elastic and ready to be stretched to the thinness required.

ravioli neri di gamberi e pesce
BLACK RAVIOLI FILLED WITH SNAPPER AND PRAWNS

RAVIOLI
1 quantity of Fresh Black Pasta Dough
    (see above)
200 g prawns, shelled and deveined
200 g snapper fillets, cleaned
Salt and pepper to taste
50 ml pure cream
1 egg, beaten

FILLING Mince prawns and snapper. Add salt, pepper and cream. Mix well and set aside till needed.

PASTA Feed the prepared pasta dough gradually through a pasta machine until you reach the lowest setting possible. Brush a strip of the rolled pasta with beaten egg. Place dollops of snapper mixture onto the dough (approximately 2 tablespoons per dollop), leaving about 4 cm between each amount. Lay another rolled pasta sheet on top and gently press any air out. Using a 3-cm fluted cutter (or a small glass), cut around each mound of filling. Continue with remaining pasta and filling. Cook ravioli in boiling salted water for 5 minutes. (This will make approximately 12–16 ravioli.)

SAUCE
100 ml Fish Stock (see page 154) (optional)
50 g butter
3 tomatoes, peeled, seeded and diced

While the ravioli are cooking, combine fish stock, butter and tomatoes in a large frying pan and cook over high heat until reduced by half. Add ravioli and toss to coat well with the sauce.

SERVES 4

John Olsen, Nude drawing,
1991, charcoal on paper

RAVIOLI NERI DI GAMBERI E PESCE

gnocchi neri alle seppie
BLACK GNOCCHI WITH CUTTLEFISH SAUCE

GNOCCHI
250 g potatoes
½ tblsp squid ink
50 g plain flour

CUTTLEFISH SAUCE
1 onion, finely diced
50 ml extra virgin olive oil
½ kg cuttlefish, cleaned
100 ml Fish Stock (see page 154)
   (optional)

Peel the potatoes and cut them into large pieces. Cover with water and boil until soft but not mushy. Drain, mash and leave to cool completely.

Mix squid ink and flour into potatoes. Do not overwork the dough. On a floured bench, roll the dough into long thin snakes (about the thickness of an average garden hose) and cut into 1-cm dumplings.

Bring a large saucepan of water to the boil, then lower the heat to a simmer. Gently place small batches of gnocchi into the water. Do not overcrowd the saucepan. As the gnocchi rise to the surface, remove them with a slotted spoon. Place cooked gnocchi in a stainless steel bowl until all gnocchi have been cooked, then add to the cuttlefish sauce.

TO MAKE SAUCE Clean cuttlefish and set aside. In a large frying pan, heat the olive oil and cook the onion on medium heat for 10 minutes without allowing it to colour. Cut the cuttlefish into small thin strips, add to the onion and cook for 3 minutes. Add stock, if desired.

Add cooked gnocchi to frying pan and return to heat. Cook for 1–2 minutes then serve.

SERVES 4

NOTE To clean cuttlefish, remove the large beak, skin and insides. Wash under running cold water and pat dry with a paper towel. We also recommend that you wear clear rubber gloves when making this gnocchi, as the squid ink will stain your skin.

tagliatelle nere ai porri con scampi alla griglia
BLACK TAGLIATELLE WITH GRILLED SCAMPI AND LEEKS

TAGLIATELLE
1 quantity of Fresh Black Pasta Dough
   (see page 66)

SAUCE
6 scampi
2 leeks, washed and diced
150 ml extra virgin olive oil
1 clove garlic, diced
Olive oil for grilling

Feed the prepared pasta dough gradually through a pasta machine until you reach the lowest setting possible. Attach the tagliatelle cutter and roll the pasta through again.

TO MAKE SAUCE Cut scampi lengthways, wash and devein, and grill on high for 2 minutes on each side. Fry leeks, olive oil and garlic over medium heat for 4 minutes.

Cook pasta in boiling water for 3 minutes and drain thoroughly. Add to leeks and toss well.

To serve, place pasta in bowls with grilled scampi on top.

SERVES 4

Ron Robertson-Swann,
Riders of the Sea, 1996, steel

TAGLIATELLE NERE AI PORRI CON SCAMPI ALLA GRIGLIA

dried pasta

spaghetti aglio olio e peperoncino
SPAGHETTI WITH GARLIC, OIL AND CHILLI

500 g spaghetti
5 tblsp extra virgin olive oil
50 g lean pancetta, chopped
2 cloves whole peeled garlic
1 hot chilli, chopped
½ bunch fresh parsley, chopped

Cook the spaghetti in boiling salted water until al dente. Meanwhile, heat the olive oil in a large frying pan. Add the pancetta, garlic and chilli and cook gently for 2 minutes until the garlic starts to colour slightly. Remove the garlic, add the drained spaghetti and toss to coat well. Add the parsley and serve immediately.

SERVES 4

spaghetti alle vongole in bianco
SPAGHETTI WITH VONGOLE

800 g vongole
6 tblsp extra virgin olive oil
1 whole clove garlic
1 hot chilli, chopped
350 g spaghetti
½ bunch fresh parsley, chopped

In a large frying pan heat 1 tablespoon of olive oil over high heat. Cook the vongole until they open (about 2 minutes). Discard any that do not open. Drain and reserve the liquid. Remove the vongole meat from two-thirds of the shells, leaving one-third intact.

In another frying pan, heat the remaining olive oil over medium heat, add the garlic and cook until light brown (about 2 minutes). Remove and discard the garlic, add the vongole and chilli to the frying pan and allow to cook for 1 minute over medium heat. Add 1 tablespoon of the reserved liquid and set aside.

Cook the spaghetti in boiling salted water until al dente. Drain thoroughly. Add spaghetti and parsley to vongole, toss well and serve immediately.

SERVES 4

Salvatore Zofrea, *Family Having Evening Meal*, 1992, woodblock

green pasta

pasta verde
FRESH GREEN PASTA DOUGH

½ bunch silverbeet (leaves only)
3 whole eggs
500 g (4 cups) plain flour
25 g cooking salt

TO PREPARE THE DOUGH Wash silverbeet then boil in salted water for 5 minutes. Refresh under cold water then squeeze in a cloth to remove excess moisture. In a blender, process silverbeet and eggs until very finely puréed.

On a clean workbench, mix flour and salt together and make a well in the centre. Place spinach mixture in the well and gradually mix in the flour with your hands until a dough forms. Knead for about 10 minutes, cover with cling film and allow to rest in the refrigerator for at least 30 minutes before using.

USING THE PASTA MACHINE Divide the dough into five balls. Flatten each ball with the palm of your hand until thin enough to fit between the rollers (approximately 1 cm).

Feed the dough through a pasta machine on the widest setting. Sprinkle the resulting strip with flour on both sides and fold into thirds. Repeat this feeding, flouring and folding 8 to 10 times, until the dough is smooth and elastic and ready to be stretched to the thinness required.

gnocchi verdi al gorgonzola e pistacchi
GREEN GNOCCHI WITH BLUE CHEESE AND PISTACHIO NUTS

GNOCCHI
½ bunch silverbeet (leaves only)
250 g potatoes
50 g plain flour

SAUCE
200 g blue vein cheese
60 ml pure cream
80 g pistachio nut kernels

Wash silverbeet then boil in salted water for 5 minutes. Refresh under cold water then squeeze in a cloth to remove excess moisture.

Peel the potatoes and cut them into large pieces. Cover with water and boil until soft but not mushy. Drain, mash and leave to cool completely.

Mix silverbeet and flour into potatoes. Do not overwork the dough. On a floured bench, roll the dough into long thin snakes (about the thickness of an average garden hose) and cut into 1-cm dumplings.

Bring a large saucepan of water to the boil, then lower the heat to a simmer. Gently place small batches of gnocchi into the water. Do not overcrowd the saucepan. As the gnocchi rise to the surface, remove them with a slotted spoon. Place cooked gnocchi in a stainless steel bowl until all gnocchi have been cooked, then add to the sauce.

TO MAKE SAUCE Melt cheese and cream in a large frying pan over medium heat, stirring occasionally.

To serve, add gnocchi to cheese sauce, toss to coat them well, then sprinkle chopped pistachio nuts on top.

SERVES 4

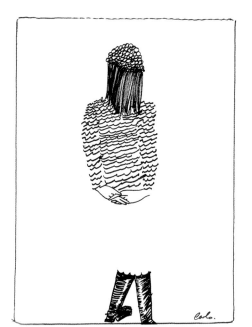

Charles Blackman,
Sketchbook drawing in
Venice, 1983

Making tagliolini >

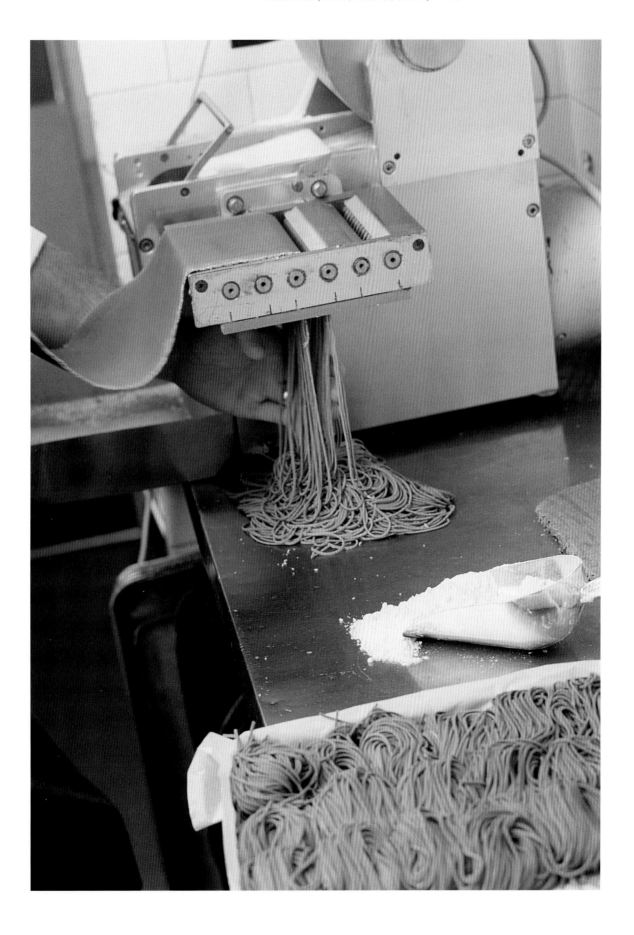

tagliolini alla granseola
GREEN TAGLIOLINI WITH BLUE SWIMMER CRAB

1 quantity of Fresh Green Pasta Dough (see page 72)
3 large blue swimmer crabs (raw)
100 g butter
1 clove garlic, finely diced
400 ml Tomato Sauce (see page 158)

PASTA Feed the prepared pasta dough gradually through a pasta machine until you reach the middle setting. Attach the tagliolini cutter and feed the pasta through again.

TO CLEAN THE CRABS Remove the claws from the bodies. Break the claws and remove the meat. Remove the heads from the bodies and take the lungs out. Break the bodies in half lengthways and squeeze the meat out. Place all meat into a colander and allow to drain for 10 minutes to remove any liquid.

TO COOK In a large, heavy-based frying pan, melt butter over medium heat. Add the drained crab meat and cook gently for 2–3 minutes. Add garlic and cook for a further 2 minutes. (Do not let the crab or the garlic colour.) Add tomato sauce, bring to the boil, then reduce heat and simmer for a further 3 minutes.

Cook the fresh tagliolini in boiling salted water for 2 minutes then drain thoroughly. Add to the sauce and toss to coat well. The pasta will absorb most of the tomato sauce. Serve immediately.

SERVES 4

TAGLIOLINI ALLA GRANSEOLA >

plain pasta

pasta bianca
FRESH WHITE PASTA DOUGH

500 g (4 cups) plain flour
25 g cooking salt
2 whole eggs
3 egg yolks

TO PREPARE THE DOUGH On a clean workbench, mix flour and salt together and make a well in the centre. In a bowl, whisk eggs and yolks together. Pour mixture into the well in the flour and gradually mix in the flour with your hands until a dough forms. Knead for about 10 minutes, cover with cling film and allow to rest in the refrigerator for at least 30 minutes before using.

USING THE PASTA MACHINE Divide the dough into five balls. Flatten each ball with the palm of your hand until thin enough to fit between the rollers (approximately 1 cm).

Feed the dough through a pasta machine on the widest setting. Sprinkle the resulting strip with flour on both sides and fold into thirds. Repeat this feeding, flouring and folding 8 to 10 times, until the dough is smooth and elastic and ready to be stretched to the thinness required.

gnocchi di patate con funghi e spinaci
POTATO GNOCCHI WITH SHIITAKE MUSHROOMS AND ENGLISH SPINACH

GNOCCHI
250 g potatoes
50 g plain flour

Peel the potatoes and cut them into large pieces. Cover with water and boil until soft but not mushy. Drain, mash and leave to cool completely.

Mix flour into potatoes. Do not overwork the dough. On a floured bench, roll the dough into long thin snakes (about the thickness of an average garden hose) and cut into 1-cm dumplings.

Bring a large saucepan of water to the boil, then lower the heat to a simmer. Gently place small batches of gnocchi into the water. Do not overcrowd the saucepan. As the gnocchi rise to the surface, remove them with a slotted spoon. Place cooked gnocchi in a stainless steel bowl until all gnocchi have been cooked, then add to the sauce.

SAUCE
100 g butter
2 punnets shiitake mushrooms, sliced
1 bunch English spinach, washed and sliced
160 g parmesan cheese, grated (more if desired)

In a frying pan, melt butter over medium heat, add sliced mushrooms and cook for 3 minutes. Add drained gnocchi and sliced spinach. Toss well to coat with butter. Sprinkle with the parmesan and serve.

SERVES 4

ABOVE: Donald Friend, Drawings, early 1970s

Colin Lanceley, *A Traveller's Tale*, 1994–95, mixed media on paper

pappardelle al coniglio e peperoni arrostiti
PAPPARDELLE WITH BRAISED RABBIT AND ROAST CAPSICUMS

SAUCE

1 white rabbit (available from good butchers)
1 onion, diced
4 cloves garlic, peeled
1 quantity of White Chicken Stock (see page 153)
60 ml extra virgin olive oil
2 Roast Capsicums (see page 34)
160 g parmesan cheese, grated (more if desired)

Cut rabbit into even pieces. Place in a baking tray with onion, garlic and chicken stock. Cover with aluminium foil and bake for 1½–2 hours at 160°C. Once rabbit is cooked, discard liquid and vegetables. Remove any bones from the rabbit. Place rabbit meat in a large pan with olive oil and sliced roast capsicums and set aside.

PAPPARDELLE

1 quantity of Fresh White Pasta Dough (see page 76)

Feed the prepared pasta dough gradually through a pasta machine until you reach the lowest setting possible. Using a sharp knife, cut the dough into strips 2 cm wide by 5 cm long. Cook pasta in boiling salted water for 2 minutes.

To serve, heat the sauce and add cooked pasta. Toss well to coat and sprinkle with parmesan.

SERVES 4

ravioli di patate e pancetta
MASHED POTATO AND PANCETTA RAVIOLI WITH CINNAMON AND POPPY-SEED BUTTER

RAVIOLI
1 quantity of Fresh White Pasta Dough (see page 76)
400 g potatoes
200 ml olive oil
1 onion, finely diced
100 g pancetta or bacon
2 egg yolks
50 g parmesan cheese, grated
½ bunch fresh continental parsley, chopped
1 egg, beaten

FILLING Peel the potatoes and cut them into large pieces. Cover with water and boil until soft but not mushy, then drain and mash.

Heat olive oil in a saucepan over low heat, add onion and chopped pancetta and cook for about 10 minutes, but do not colour. Add to mashed potato and leave to cool slightly. Add egg yolks, parmesan and parsley and leave to cool completely.

PASTA Feed the prepared pasta dough gradually through a pasta machine until you reach the lowest setting possible. Brush a strip of the rolled pasta with beaten egg. Place 2 tablespoonfuls of potato mixture onto the dough, leaving about 4 cm between each amount. Lay another rolled pasta sheet on top and gently press any air out. Using a 3-cm fluted cutter (or a small glass), cut around each mound of filling. Continue with remaining pasta and filling. Cook ravioli in boiling salted water for 5 minutes. (This will make approximately 12–16 ravioli.)

SAUCE
100 g butter
1/2 tsp cinnamon
1 tsp poppy seeds
Parmesan cheese, shaved, to serve

While ravioli are cooking, melt butter in a large frying pan over low heat. Add cinnamon and poppy seeds. Add ravioli, toss to coat well and serve immediately with shaved parmesan.

SERVES 4

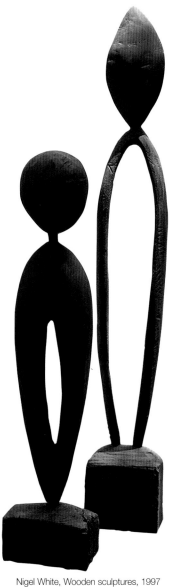

Nigel White, Wooden sculptures, 1997

RAVIOLI DI PATATE E PANCETTA >

ravioli di spinaci e ricotta al burro fuso e salvia
SPINACH AND RICOTTA RAVIOLI WITH BURNT BUTTER AND SAGE

RAVIOLI
1 quantity of Fresh White Pasta Dough
  (see page 76)
3 bunches English spinach
3 tsp nutmeg
400 g ricotta cheese
300 g parmesan cheese, grated

SAUCE
100 g butter
2 tsp fresh sage, chopped

FILLING Blanch spinach in boiling salted water. Using a chef's knife, cut into fine strips. In a large bowl, combine spinach, nutmeg, ricotta and 200 g of the parmesan and allow to cool completely.

PASTA Feed the prepared pasta dough gradually through a pasta machine until you reach the lowest setting possible. Brush a strip of the rolled pasta with beaten egg. Place 2 tablespoonfuls of ricotta mixture onto the dough, leaving about 4 cm between each amount. Lay another rolled pasta sheet on top and gently press any air out. Using a 3-cm fluted cutter (or a small glass), cut around each mound of filling. Continue with remaining pasta and filling. Cook ravioli in boiling salted water for 5 minutes. (This will make approximately 12–16 ravioli.)

TO MAKE SAUCE While ravioli are cooking, melt butter in a large frying pan over medium heat. Cook for 3–4 minutes until it is a nut-brown colour. Add sage and cooked ravioli and toss well to coat.

To serve, divide ravioli among serving plates with some of the burnt butter, sprinkle with the remaining parmesan and serve.

SERVES 4

stracci al caprino e pomodoro
RAG PASTA WITH DICED TOMATOES, MIXED HERBS AND GOAT'S CHEESE

1 quantity of Fresh White Pasta Dough
  (see page 76)
4 vine-ripened tomatoes, skinned and
  diced
150 ml extra virgin olive oil
2 tsp fresh tarragon, chopped

2 tsp fresh chervil, chopped
2 tsp fresh basil, chopped
2 tsp fresh parsley, chopped
150 g (1 log) Kryton goat's cheese,
  sliced approximately ½ cm thick

Feed the prepared pasta dough gradually through a pasta machine until you reach the lowest setting possible. With a sharp knife, cut dough into rag shapes, keeping them similar in size. Cook pasta in boiling salted water for 2 minutes.

Combine tomatoes, olive oil and mixed herbs in a large bowl. Add pasta and toss well to coat. On serving plates, arrange alternate layers of pasta and goat's cheese slices. Serve immediately to prevent it from collapsing.

SERVES 4

NOTE If Kryton goat's cheese is unavailable, any good quality mild, creamy goat's cheese will do.

OPPOSITE TOP:
John Coburn, *Winter's Night*, 1992, watercolour on paper

OPPOSITE BOTTOM:
John Coburn, *San Marco*, 1997, watercolour on paper

porcini pasta

pasta di porcini
FRESH PORCINI MUSHROOM PASTA DOUGH

50 g dried porcini mushrooms
3 whole eggs
500 g (4 cups) plain flour
25 g cooking salt

Soak porcini mushrooms in boiling water for 30 minutes, then drain. In a blender, process mushrooms and eggs until finely puréed.

TO PREPARE THE DOUGH On a clean workbench, mix flour and salt together and make a well in the centre. Add porcini mixture to the well and gradually mix in the flour with your hands until a dough forms. Knead for about 10 minutes, cover with cling film and allow to rest in the refrigerator for at least 30 minutes before using.

USING THE PASTA MACHINE Divide the dough into five balls. Flatten each ball with the palm of your hand until thin enough to fit between the rollers (approximately 1 cm).

Feed the dough through a pasta machine on the widest setting. Sprinkle the resulting strip with flour on both sides and fold into thirds. Repeat this feeding, flouring and folding 8 to 10 times, until the dough is smooth and elastic and ready to be stretched to the thinness required.

linguine di porcini agli spinaci e scamorza
PORCINI MUSHROOM LINGUINE WITH SCAMORZA CHEESE AND ENGLISH SPINACH

1 quantity of Fresh Porcini Mushroom Pasta Dough (see above)
100 ml White Chicken Stock (see page 153)
½ bunch English spinach, sliced
100 g Scamorza cheese, cut into 1-cm cubes

Feed the prepared pasta dough gradually through a pasta machine until you reach the second lowest setting. Attach the linguine cutter to the machine and roll pasta through again. Cook pasta in boiling salted water for 2 minutes.

While pasta is cooking, bring stock to the boil in a stainless steel frying pan. Add drained pasta, sliced spinach and Scamorza cheese and mix with a fork until the cheese is slightly melted.

SERVES 4

NOTE Scamorza is a smoked mozzarella cheese.

Jason Benjamin, Ceramic plate, 1998

pappardelle di porcini ai petti di quaglia e salvia
PORCINI MUSHROOM PAPPARDELLE WITH GRILLED QUAIL BREAST AND SAGE

PASTA
1 quantity of Fresh Porcini Mushroom Pasta Dough (see page 82)

Feed the prepared pasta dough gradually through a pasta machine until you reach the lowest setting possible. Using a sharp knife, cut the dough into strips 2 cm wide by 5 cm long.

SAUCE
500 ml Brown Chicken Stock (see page 153) (optional)
4 breasts of quail
½ bunch fresh sage, chopped
Olive oil for grilling
160 g parmesan cheese, grated (more if desired)

In a saucepan, bring stock to the boil, then reduce heat and simmer until reduced by half.

Grill quail breasts on medium to high for 3 minutes on each side.

While the quail breasts are cooking, boil pasta in salted water for 2 minutes. Drain and add pasta and sage to stock. Sprinkle with parmesan and mix well.

To serve, top cooked pasta with quail breast.

SERVES 4

NOTE If you do not want to use the stock, you can toss the pappardelle in 100 g of melted butter instead.

Jeffrey Makin, Ceramic plate, 1998

pasta allo zafferano
FRESH SAFFRON PASTA DOUGH

500 g (4 cups) plain flour
25 g cooking salt
1 tsp saffron threads
2 whole eggs
3 egg yolks

TO PREPARE THE DOUGH On a clean workbench, mix flour and salt together and make a well in the centre. In a mortar and pestle, crush the saffron threads. In a bowl, whisk eggs, yolks and saffron together. Add saffron mixture to the well in the flour, gradually mixing flour into eggs with your hands until a dough forms. Knead for about 10 minutes, cover with cling film and allow to rest in the refrigerator for at least 30 minutes before using.

USING THE PASTA MACHINE Divide the dough into five balls. Flatten each ball with the palm of your hand until thin enough to fit between the rollers (approximately 1 cm).

Feed the dough through a pasta machine on the widest setting. Sprinkle the resulting strip with flour on both sides and fold into thirds. Repeat this feeding, flouring and folding 8 to 10 times, until the dough is smooth and elastic and ready to be stretched to the thinness required.

saffron pasta

gnocchi alle cozze e punte di asparagi
SAFFRON GNOCCHI WITH MUSSELS AND ASPARAGUS TIPS

GNOCCHI
250 g potatoes
2 tsp saffron threads
50 g plain flour
12 spears of asparagus, tips only

SAUCE
1 tblsp olive oil
6 garlic cloves, peeled and roughly chopped
1 kg Tasmanian mussels, washed
50 g unsalted butter, chopped

Peel the potatoes and cut them into large pieces. Cover with water and boil until soft but not mushy. Drain, mash and leave to cool completely.

Mix saffron and flour into potatoes. Do not overwork the dough. On a floured bench, roll the dough into long thin snakes (about the thickness of an average garden hose) and cut into 1-cm dumplings.

Bring a large pan of water to the boil, then lower the heat to a simmer. Gently place small batches of the gnocchi and asparagus into the water. Do not overcrowd the saucepan. As the gnocchi rise to the surface, remove them and the asparagus with a slotted spoon. Place cooked gnocchi and asparagus in a stainless steel bowl until all gnocchi and asparagus have been cooked, then add to the mussel sauce.

TO MAKE SAUCE Heat the olive oil in a large saucepan over medium heat. Add garlic and mussels, cover and cook for 3 minutes or until opened. Discard any that do not open. Remove mussel meat from the shells and trim off any beards that the meat may have. Strain the cooking juices and reserve.

Place mussel juices and butter in a frying pan and bring to the boil. Add gnocchi, mussel meat and asparagus. Toss to coat the gnocchi well with the sauce. Serve immediately.

SERVES 4

Salvatore Zofrea, *Ballerina*, 1988, crayon

tagliatelle ai fiori di zucchini, pomodoro e basilico
SAFFRON TAGLIATELLE WITH ZUCCHINI FLOWERS, DICED TOMATOES AND BASIL

TAGLIATELLE
1 quantity of Fresh Saffron Pasta Dough (see page 83)

Feed the prepared pasta dough gradually through a pasta machine until you reach the lowest setting possible. Attach the tagliatelle cutter and roll the pasta through again.

SAUCE
16 zucchini flowers
120 ml extra virgin olive oil
3 tomatoes, peeled, seeded and diced
3 tsp fresh basil, chopped

Remove and discard the stigma and stem from the zucchini flowers. Heat the olive oil in a frying pan, add flowers and diced tomatoes and simmer for 3 minutes.

While flowers and tomatoes are simmering, boil pasta in salted water for 2 minutes. Drain thoroughly, then add to frying pan with other ingredients. Add basil, toss well but gently, and serve.

SERVES 4

< TAGLIATELLE AI FIORI DI ZUCCHINI, POMODORO E BASILICO

risotti

risotto ai fiori di zucchini
SAFFRON AND ZUCCHINI-FLOWER RISOTTO

30 zucchini flowers
200 g butter, diced
2 onions, finely diced
½ tsp saffron threads
300 g arborio rice
1 ltr White Chicken Stock (see page 153), boiling
160 g parmesan cheese, grated

Remove and discard stigma and stem from zucchini flowers. Chop flowers roughly.

Melt half the butter in a large saucepan, add onions and cook over low heat for 15 minutes. Add saffron and rice to onions and stir for at least 5 minutes to ensure that all the grains are coated. Turn up the heat slightly and add just enough hot stock to cover the rice. Stir the rice until it has absorbed all the stock. Repeat this process for 15–20 minutes, until nearly all the stock has been absorbed by the rice and the rice is a wonderful yellow colour from the saffron. Add zucchini flowers and leave to wilt for 1 minute. Add remaining butter and parmesan and mix thoroughly. (This last operation of risotto-making is called 'mantecare'.) Serve immediately.

SERVES 4

risotto ai funghi porcini
PORCINI MUSHROOM RISOTTO

½ cup dried porcini mushrooms
80 ml olive oil for cooking
3 onions, peeled and finely diced
250 g button mushrooms, roughly chopped
200 g butter, diced
300 g arborio rice
1 ltr White Veal Stock (see page 153), boiling
150 g parmesan cheese, grated

Before starting this dish, soak the porcini mushrooms in hot water for 30 minutes.

Heat some olive oil in a heavy-based saucepan, add 1 of the diced onions, and cook gently for 5 minutes. Drain porcini mushrooms and chop roughly. Add porcini and button mushrooms to pan and cook over medium heat for 20 minutes.

Melt half the butter in a large saucepan, add the remaining onions and cook over low heat for 15 minutes. Add rice to onions and stir for at least 5 minutes to ensure that all the grains are coated. Turn up the heat slightly and add just enough hot stock to cover the rice. Stir the rice until it has absorbed all the stock. Repeat this process for 15–20 minutes, until nearly all the stock has been absorbed by the rice. Add cooked mushrooms, remaining butter and parmesan and mix thoroughly. Serve immediately.

SERVES 4

Jeffrey Makin, *Bridal Veil Falls*,
1996, oil on canvas >

Vivienne Wheeler,
Togs' Castlemaine, 1994,
oil on board

risotto al crescione e taleggio
WATERCRESS AND TALEGGIO RISOTTO

1 bunch watercress
150 g Taleggio cheese
200 g butter
2 onions, finely diced
300 g arborio rice
1 ltr White Chicken Stock (see page 153), boiling
150g parmesan cheese, grated

Wash and dry watercress and remove all stems. Remove rind from Taleggio and cut into 2-cm dice. Set aside with watercress.

Melt half the butter in a large saucepan, add onions and cook over low heat for 15 minutes. Add rice to onions and stir for at least 5 minutes to ensure that all the grains are coated. Turn up the heat slightly and add just enough hot stock to cover the rice. Stir the rice until it has absorbed all the stock. Repeat this process for 15–20 minutes, until nearly all the stock has been absorbed by the rice. Add watercress leaves, Taleggio, butter and parmesan. Mix thoroughly. Serve immediately.

SERVES 4

NOTE Taleggio cheese is a soft-textured northern Italian cheese with a fruity, aromatic flavour which is increasingly available in Australia. If it is unavailable, you can use a dry mozzarella as a substitute, however the flavours will be different.

risotto al radicchio e basilico
RADICCHIO AND BASIL RISOTTO

200 g butter, diced
2 onions, finely diced
300 g arborio rice
1 ltr White Veal Stock (see page 153), boiling
1 head of red-leaf radicchio, washed and sliced
½ bunch fresh basil, finely sliced
150 g parmesan cheese, grated

Melt half the butter in a large saucepan, add onions and cook over low heat for 15 minutes. Add rice to onions and stir for at least 5 minutes to ensure that all the grains are coated. Turn up the heat slightly and add just enough hot stock to cover the rice. Stir the rice until it has absorbed all the stock. Repeat this process for 15–20 minutes, until nearly all the stock has been absorbed by the rice. Add sliced radicchio and basil, leave to wilt for 1 minute, then add remaining butter and parmesan. Mix thoroughly. Serve immediately.

SERVES 4

zuppe

lattughe ripiene in brodo
CHICKEN BROTH WITH LETTUCE PARCELS

LETTUCE PARCELS
250 g chicken mince
60 g mascarpone cheese
50 g ricotta cheese
2 egg yolks
1 iceberg lettuce
Salt and pepper to taste

In a large bowl, combine mince, both cheeses and egg yolks. Blanch separated iceberg lettuce leaves in boiling salted water. Dry lettuce and lay leaves on bench. Place tablespoonfuls of chicken mixture on lettuce leaves and fold the leaves to make parcels the size of matchboxes.

STOCK
500 ml White Chicken Stock (see page 153)
500 ml Brown Chicken Stock (see page 153)
½ large carrot, peeled
1 stick celery
½ leek, cleaned
1 small zucchini

Cut all vegetables into julienne strips 5 cm by 2 mm. In a large saucepan, bring chicken stocks to the boil. Reduce heat, add julienned vegetables and prepared lettuce parcels and simmer for 2 minutes. Season with salt and pepper and serve.

SERVES 5

zuppa di fagioli borlotti e radicchio
BORLOTTI BEAN AND RADICCHIO SOUP

375 g dried borlotti beans
1 head garlic, cut in half
1 onion, peeled and chopped
1 carrot, peeled and chopped
1 stick celery, peeled and chopped
8 tblsp extra virgin olive oil
500 ml White Chicken Stock (see page 153)
3 heads red-leaf radicchio

Before cooking, soak borlotti beans for 10–12 hours in cold water then drain beans and discard soaking water.

In a medium saucepan, place borlotti beans, garlic and enough water to cover. Cook on medium heat for about 40 minutes. Discard cooking water and garlic and purée half the beans.

In a large pot, heat 2 tablespoons of the olive oil over low heat and sweat the onion, carrot and celery for 10 minutes or until tender. Add chicken stock and bring to the boil. Add whole and puréed beans, reduce heat and simmer for 30 minutes, then add salt and pepper.

To serve, slice radicchio very finely, dress with 2 tablespoons of the olive oil and place on top of soup. Drizzle the rest of the olive oil around the radicchio.

SERVES 6

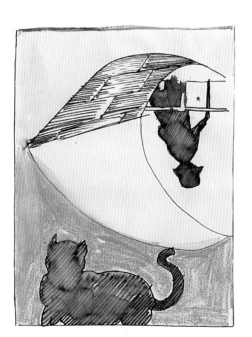

Charles Blackman,
Sketchbook drawing in
Venice, 1983

zuppa di fagioli, pancetta e funghi porcini
WHITE BEAN, PANCETTA AND PORCINI MUSHROOM SOUP

375 g dried haricot beans
1 cup dried porcini mushrooms
1 head garlic, cut in half
2 tblsp olive oil
1 onion, peeled and finely diced

80 g flat pancetta, finely diced
500 ml White Chicken Stock (see
   page 153)
180 g parmesan cheese, grated
6 slices of Italian bread, toasted

Before cooking, soak haricot beans in cold water for 10–12 hours then drain beans and discard soaking water.

Soak the porcini mushrooms in hot water for 30 minutes, then drain and chop.

In a medium saucepan, place haricot beans, garlic and enough water to cover. Cook over medium heat for about 30 minutes or until beans are tender but not mushy. Drain beans, discarding the cooking water. Purée one-third of the beans.

In a large pot, heat olive oil and sweat onion, pancetta and porcini mushrooms over low heat until softened but not coloured. Add chicken stock and whole and puréed haricot beans. Bring to the boil, reduce heat and simmer for about 20 minutes.

To serve, sprinkle with the parmesan and serve with some toasted Italian bread.

SERVES 6

zuppa di lenticchie con pelle di zampone croccante
LENTIL SOUP WITH CRISPY PIGS' TROTTERS

2 pigs' trotters
1 onion, chopped
1 carrot, chopped
1 stick celery, chopped
500 ml Brown Veal Stock (see page 153)

SOUP
50 ml extra virgin olive oil
1 onion, finely diced
400 g du Puy lentils
800 ml White Chicken Stock (see
   page 153)

Scrape pigs' trotters with a knife to remove any hair from the feet. Place in a medium-sized roasting pan with vegetables and stock. Cover with aluminium foil and roast at 180°C for 3 hours.

Remove skin from the bone, discard bone and flesh, then chop skin into small pieces.

In a small frying pan, heat pieces of trotters for about 2–3 minutes on each side. (The pieces will stick together.) Chop again and place on paper towel to drain.

TO MAKE SOUP In a large saucepan, heat olive oil over low heat and sweat onion until transparent but not coloured. Add lentils and cook for about 4 minutes. Add chicken stock, bring to the boil, reduce heat and simmer for 20–30 minutes.

Remove soup from heat and purée one-third of the cooked lentils. Return puréed lentils to the pot, return pot to heat and bring to the boil just before serving.

To serve, ladle into bowls and top with some of the crispy skin from the pigs' trotters.

SERVES 6

NOTE Du Puy lentils are a French lentil and can be cooked without prior soaking. They also tend to hold their shape better than normal lentils. If du Puy lentils are unavailable, normal brown lentils will do, but remember to soak them before cooking and that they may take a little longer to cook.

Ken Johnson, Ceramic plate, 1998

Deruta hand-painted convent floor tiles

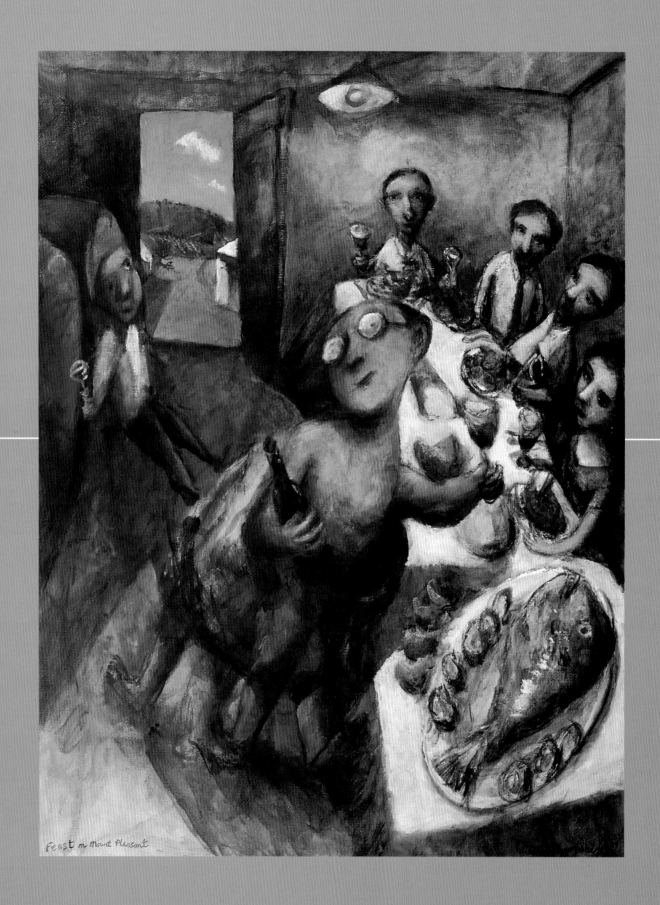

Feast on Mount Pleasant

pesce

Everyone has a favourite restaurant — mine is Lucio's.

Cities around the world boast restaurants that become legendary because they are where artists and writers meet and where the movers and shakers of society have chosen to eat. Lucio's is of that calibre.

It's not hard to understand why, either. Fuelled by the excellent food and art on the walls, the atmosphere is always lively. On entering the restaurant you feel a tingle of anticipation for an enjoyable evening ahead, one that will engage all your senses.

Lucio has a way of making you feel immediately at home, somehow relaxed, receptive. His 'team' of waiters, surely the best in Sydney, conduct themselves with a blend of friendliness and skilful service that seems effortless — such is their ability.

Finally, of course, a restaurant will survive on the excellence of its food. Lucio's secret is fundamental to all great establishments — the best ingredients served fresh and simply, having a balance of tastes with nothing overwhelming anything else.

Living in France for half the year, I have to admit to missing Lucio's. Surrounded as I am by many reputedly great restaurants, I still dream of returning to Sydney to savour the Salmon Tartare with Sevruga Caviar or the Grilled Figs with Mushrooms, or the Green Tagliolini with Blue Swimmer Crab. To follow, possibly the Duck, the Rack of Lamb, or maybe the Veal Medallions he does so well. Just writing this has made me hungry as I picture it all in my mind.

Like a migratory bird come late September, I head for home, for the sunshine, the warmth and Lucio's!

FRED CRESS

aguglie al forno con prezzemolo, pomodori secchi e borlotti

BAKED GARFISH WITH PARSLEY, OVEN-DRIED TOMATOES AND FRESH BORLOTTI BEANS

360 g fresh borlotti beans
30 garfish
220 ml extra virgin olive oil
120 g Oven-Dried Tomatoes (see page 158)
1 bunch fresh flat-leaf parsley, chopped

Peel and steam borlotti beans for 15 minutes. Meanwhile, scale and fillet the garfish, taking care to remove all bones. Place fish on an oven tray, drizzle with 100 ml of the olive oil, then bake in a pre-heated oven for 8–10 minutes at 200°C.

Roughly chop the oven-dried tomatoes and combine in a bowl with cooked beans, parsley and olive oil.

To serve, place bean mixture on 6 individual plates and top with grilled fish.

SERVES 6

dentice al forno con la cicoria

BABY SNAPPER FILLETS WITH WILTED CHICORY AND SPRING ONIONS

3 bunches spring onions
200 ml olive oil
6 baby snapper, filleted
1 bunch fresh chicory, washed
60 ml extra virgin olive oil for drizzling

Peel and slice spring onions. Heat half the olive oil in a saucepan over low heat, add the spring onions, cover and cook for 20 minutes, stirring occasionally.

Remove all bones from snapper fillets and place on a large oven tray with the remaining olive oil. Bake at 180°C for 15 minutes.

Add chicory to spring onions to wilt it slightly.

To serve, arrange spring onions and chicory on serving plates and top with the fish. Drizzle with extra virgin olive oil.

SERVES 6

< AGUGLIE AL FORNO CON PREZZEMOLO,
  POMODORI SECCHI E BORLOTTI

John Olsen, Ceramic plate, 1998

calamari alla griglia con couscous, pancetta e peperoncino

GRILLED BABY CALAMARI WITH COUSCOUS, PANCETTA AND CHILLIES

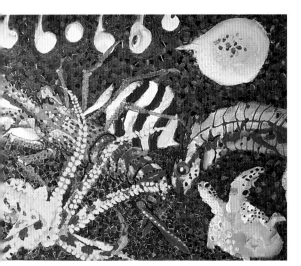

Frank Hodgkinson, View of
underbar panels (detail),
1998, oil on canvas

300 g couscous
500 ml White Chicken Stock (see page 153), boiling
100 g pancetta (or bacon)
100 g unsalted butter
1.5 kg baby calamari
Olive oil for grilling
200 g (1½ cups) anahem chillies (or other mild chillies), sliced
100 ml extra virgin olive oil

Place couscous in a large bowl, pour boiling stock over, ensuring that the couscous is covered by the stock, and allow to stand for 15 minutes.

Cut pancetta into small pieces. Over medium heat, melt the butter. Add pancetta and cook until soft. Add pancetta to couscous, raking the couscous with a fork to loosen it.

Clean the calamari, retaining the tentacles. Place the calamari on a hot grill, sprinkle with a little olive oil, salt and pepper, and cook for about 5 minutes.

In another bowl, combine the sliced chillies, calamari and extra virgin olive oil. Toss well and serve with couscous.

SERVES 6

cozze alla marinara

CLASSIC MUSSELS

2 kg mussels
8 tblsp extra virgin olive oil
3 cloves garlic, crushed
1 chilli, chopped
160 ml dry white wine
½ bunch fresh parsley, chopped
Juice of 1 lemon
8 slices of Basic Bruschetta (see page 26)

Clean and wash the mussels under running water. Heat the oil in a large pan, add the garlic and cook over low heat until it is just beginning to colour. Add the chilli, mussels and wine. Mix well for 5 minutes until all the shells have opened. Discard any shells that do not open. Add the parsley and lemon juice. Mix well and serve with the bruschetta.

SERVES 4

CALAMARI ALLA GRIGLIA CON COUSCOUS,
PANCETTA E PEPERONCINO >

filetti di san pietro con puré di patate e condimento
GRILLED JOHN DORY FILLETS WITH MASHED POTATOES AND CONDIMENT

6 large desirée potatoes, peeled
60 g butter
60 ml pure cream
6 John Dory fillets (approximately 250 g each)
Olive oil for grilling
Salt and pepper to taste
¾ cup Mixed Capsicum and Red Wine Vinegar Condiment (see page 150)

In a medium-sized pot, boil the potatoes. Once cooked, drain and allow to sit in a colander for 5 minutes to dry a little, then mash with the butter and cream.

Skin the John Dory, brush with olive oil and grill on high for 6 minutes on each side. Season with salt and pepper.

To serve, place the mashed potato in the centre of six plates, top with the fish and surround with condiment.

SERVES 6

Ken Johnson, *Mask*,
1997, mixed media

filetti di aguglie con fagiolini e noci
GRILLED GARFISH WITH STRING BEANS AND WALNUTS

30 garfish
Olive oil for grilling
300 g green beans
300 g yellow wax beans
180 g (1½ cups) walnut pieces
½ cup Lemon Juice Olive Oil (see page 156)

Scale and fillet the garfish, taking care to remove all bones. Brush fish with a little olive oil and grill on high for 3 minutes on each side.

Top and tail green and yellow beans and submerge in boiling salted water for about 4 minutes. Drain and toss in a bowl with walnuts and lemon juice olive oil.

To serve, arrange beans and walnuts on serving plates and top with cooked fish.

SERVES 6

FILETTI DI SAN PIETRO CON PURÉ DI PATATE
< E CONDIMENTO

dentice al forno con patate e olive nere
BAKED SNAPPER FILLET WITH THINLY SLICED POTATOES AND BLACK OLIVES

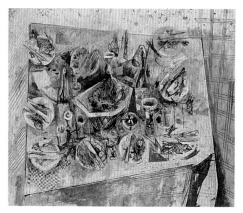

Victor Rubin, *La Dolce Vita*,
1988, oil on canvas

6 desirée potatoes
120 g unsalted butter, diced
60 g black olives, pitted and chopped
2 sprigs fresh rosemary
Salt and pepper to taste
1½-kg piece snapper or 6 large snapper fillets (approximately 250 g each)

Peel and wash the potatoes. Using a large knife, slice them as thinly as possible.
Spread potatoes on a large baking tray and add butter, black olives and rosemary.
Sprinkle with salt and pepper to taste. Sprinkle a little water over the top of the potatoes
and bake at 220°C for about 15 minutes. Cut the snapper into 6 even pieces, place on
top of the potatoes and bake for a further 10 minutes.

SERVES 6

filetti di merluzzo con vongole e zafferano
BLUE-EYE COD FILLETS BAKED WITH SAFFRON AND VONGOLE

600 g vongole
50 ml olive oil
6 cloves garlic
6 large blue-eye cod fillets (approximately 200 g each)
6 small pinches saffron threads
100 ml fish stock
100 g unsalted butter

Wash vongole thoroughly, making sure all sand is removed. In a large pot, heat olive oil
over high heat. When almost at smoking point, add vongole and garlic. Cover and leave
for about 5 minutes or until all shells are opened. Discard any shells that do not open
after 5 minutes. Remove vongole from pot and allow to cool.

Cut cod into 6 even pieces and place in a high-sided baking tray. Add saffron and fish
stock and bake at 220°C for 10–12 minutes or until the fish starts to separate into
flakes. Drain the liquid into a saucepan, bring to the boil, add vongole and diced butter.
Boil until the liquid thickens, then pour over the fish.

SERVES 6

FILETTI DI MERLUZZO CON VONGOLE
E ZAFFERANO >

filetti di triglie con sedano e salsa piccante
BAKED RED MULLET WITH PIQUANT SAUCE

18 whole red mullet (approximately 10 cm long)
200 ml extra virgin olive oil
Salt and pepper to taste

1 onion, finely diced
6 sticks celery, cut into 1-cm dice
¾ cup Piquant Sauce (see page 150)
Chives, chopped (optional)

Scale, gut and fillet the red mullet. Place on a baking tray with half of the olive oil and the salt and pepper.

In a saucepan over low heat, combine the remaining olive oil, diced onions and celery. Cover and cook for 20 minutes. Meanwhile, bake red mullet at 220°C for 5–6 minutes.

To serve, place onion and celery mixture on 6 plates, top with fish, and spoon piquant sauce over the top. Garnish with chopped chives if desired.

SERVES 6

filetti di trota con spinaci e pomodori
BAKED RAINBOW TROUT FILLETS WITH SPINACH AND TOMATOES

2 bunches English spinach
6 rainbow trout (approximately 250 g each)
220 ml extra virgin olive oil
6 vine-ripened tomatoes, diced

Wash spinach and blanch in salted water. Squeeze dry.

Scale and fillet the trout, removing all bones but leaving the tails on to act as a hinge. Place trout in a large baking tray. Peel the top fillets back. Spread spinach on one cut side of each fish and sprinkle with olive oil. Fold over the top fillets so that each trout looks like a whole fish with no head. Bake at 180°C for 15 minutes.

To serve, dress diced tomatoes with olive oil and spoon over the fish.

SERVES 6

Colin Lanceley, Ceramic plate, 1998

pesce al cartoccio
FISH IN FOIL

6 baby snapper, filleted
6 cloves garlic
6 sprigs fresh rosemary

Juice of 3–4 lemons (120 ml)
120 ml extra virgin olive oil
Salt and pepper to taste

Place each snapper fillet on a piece of aluminium foil. To each, add 1 clove garlic, 1 sprig rosemary, and a sprinkle of lemon juice, olive oil, salt and pepper. Close the foil over to make parcels and bake for 20 minutes at 200°C.

To serve, arrange on plates and pour some of the cooking juices over the top.

SERVES 6

< FILETTI DI TRIGLIE CON SEDANO E SALSA PICCANTE

PESCE AL SALE

pesce al sale
FISH IN ROCK SALT

4 kg rock salt
500 g (4 cups) plain flour
150 ml water
1 whole snapper (approximately 2 kg), cleaned
3 sprigs fresh rosemary
4 tomatoes, peeled, seeded and diced
120 ml Lemon Juice Olive Oil (see page 156)
½ bunch fresh parsley, chopped

In a large bowl, mix the rock salt, plain flour and water together to form a paste. Place rosemary sprigs inside the fish. Place fish in a large, flat baking tray and cover it completely with the salt paste to seal it. Bake at 220°C for 45–50 minutes or until the salt mixture becomes slightly coloured.

Meanwhile, mix the diced tomatoes with the lemon juice olive oil and set it aside.

Once the fish is cooked, break open the salt crust with a hammer, or if you are lucky it may lift off as a lid. Fillet the fish and transfer it to a serving platter.

To serve, top the fish with the diced tomato mix and sprinkle with some freshly chopped parsley.

SERVES 4

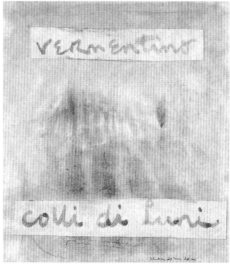

Ken Johnson, white wine label, 'Vermentino'

pesce alla griglia
BARRAMUNDI FILLETS WITH SHAVED FENNEL AND PARMESAN

1½ kg barramundi fillet (wild-caught if possible)
Olive oil for grilling
2 bulbs fennel
120 g (1¼ cup) parmesan cheese, shaved
½ bunch fresh continental parsley, chopped
120 ml Lemon Juice Olive Oil (see page 156)

Cut fish into 6 even pieces, brush with olive oil and grill on medium to high for about 5 minutes on each side. (If using wild-caught fish, the fillets may need longer, so do not have the grill too hot or the fish will dry out.)

Peel the outer layer off the fennel. Slice fennel very finely with a sharp knife. In a large bowl, combine fennel, parmesan and parsley. Add lemon juice olive oil and toss well.

To serve, arrange fish on plates and top with fennel mixture.

SERVES 6

Lucio and Giorgio serving Pesce al Sale

pesce spada con capperi, pinoli e olive
SWORDFISH WITH CAPERS, PINENUTS AND OLIVES

⅔ cup extra virgin olive oil
4 swordfish steaks (approximately 200 g each)
200 ml dry white wine
1 tblsp capers

1 tblsp pinenuts
½ bunch oregano, chopped
½ bunch parsley, chopped
80 g (½ cup) black olives

Gently heat the olive oil in a large frying pan and cook the fish for 2 minutes on each side. Add the wine and reduce for 1 minute. Add the capers, pinenuts, oregano, parsley and olives. Cook for a further 4 minutes, shaking the pan occasionally so that the fish does not stick.

To serve, arrange each swordfish steak on a plate and pour over the sauce.

SERVES 4

pesce spada con puré di olive verdi
GRILLED SWORDFISH WITH GREEN OLIVE SALSA

180 g green olives, pitted
12 French eschallots, peeled
100 ml extra virgin olive oil
30 ml red wine vinegar

1.2-kg piece swordfish or 6 swordfish steaks (approximately 200 g each)
Olive oil for grilling
Salt and pepper to taste

Chop olives and eschallots very finely. In a large bowl, combine with extra virgin olive oil and vinegar and mix well.

Cut the swordfish into 6 even steaks. Brush with olive oil, sprinkle with salt and pepper and grill on high for 6 minutes on each side. Serve with olive salsa on the side.

SERVES 6

trancia di tonno pepato con finocchio brasato
PEPPERED YELLOW-FIN TUNA WITH BRAISED FENNEL

3 fennel bulbs
100 ml olive oil
150 ml White Chicken Stock (see page 153)

1.2-kg piece yellow-fin tuna or 6 tuna steaks (approximately 200 g each)
½ bunch fresh thyme
60 g peppercorns, crushed

Peel and discard the outer leaves of fennel. Cut fennel into thin wedges. Heat 80 ml of the olive oil over medium heat, add fennel, reduce heat and cook for 10 minutes, stirring occasionally. Add stock and cook for a further 15 minutes or until the fennel is tender but not mushy.

Cut tuna into 6 even slices, discarding any blood from the fish. Brush with the remaining olive oil and sprinkle thyme and crushed peppercorns on both sides. Grill on high for about 5 minutes on each side, making sure the centre of the tuna is still very pink.

To serve, arrange the braised fennel on plates and top with the tuna.

SERVES 6

Frank Hodgkinson, Ceramic plate, 1998

Frank Hodgkinson, *Crayfish,
Polyps and Sweetlips*, 1989,
mixed media

zuppa di pesce
FISH SOUP

500 g cuttlefish
500 g calamari
500 g baby octopus
500 g black mussels
4 small cutlets of any fish
4 small red mullet
100 ml extra virgin olive oil
2 garlic cloves, peeled and chopped
1 chilli, chopped
160 ml dry white wine
4 ripe tomatoes, peeled, seeded and diced
½ bunch fresh parsley, chopped
8 slices of Basic Bruschetta (see page 26)

Clean all the seafood and cut the cuttlefish, calamari and octopus into strips. If you are not sure about how to clean the seafood, you can ask your fishmonger to do it for you.

In a large saucepan, heat the olive oil over low heat, add the garlic and chilli and cook for 4 minutes. Do not let the garlic colour. Add the cuttlefish, calamari and octopus and cook on medium heat for about 9 minutes. Add the white wine and allow it to evaporate. Add the tomatoes, cover, and cook for about 10 minutes. Add the fish, toss gently to cover it with the sauce and cook for about 6 minutes. Add the mussels and cook until they open. Discard any shells that do not open after 5 minutes. Sprinkle with parsley and mix gently, taking care not to break up the fish fillets.

Serve in individual plates or a serving platter in the middle of the table, with the bruschetta.

SERVES 4

OPPOSITE: Artists' lunch (left to right) John Coburn, Fred Cress, John Beard, Tim Storrier, Lucio, Garry Shead, Tom Lowenstein and John Olsen

square cut shoulder
1 9 9 9

carne

There is only one Lucio's.

   The very name of the place, even after only fifteen years in Sydney, evokes not simply a cuisine but a way of being. The secret of Lucio's is not only its extraordinary food and wide-ranging cellar but also its relaxed atmosphere in which high spirits flow exuberantly. Lucio is this spirit and he delivers it in true Ligurian tradition through his Italian province's distinctive dishes and wines. His is far more than mere charm. It is professionalism of a particularly delicate kind. Lucio's love of art, his friendship with artists, his embracing warmth and bonhomie place his restaurant apart from others.

FRANK HODGKINSON

PAGE 114 Tim Storrier, *Square Cut Shoulder*, 1999, acrylic on board

agnello arrosto con puré di topinambour
ROAST LAMB WITH PURÉE OF JERUSALEM ARTICHOKES

400 g desiree potatoes
200 g Jerusalem artichokes
Olive oil for frying
4 lamb loins, boneless (approximately 200 g each)
4 tomatoes, peeled and seeded
80 ml extra virgin olive oil
50 g butter
80 ml pure cream

Peel and chop the potatoes and artichokes, cutting the potatoes twice the size of the artichokes. In a saucepan, cover with water, bring to the boil and cook until soft. Put through a food mill and set aside.

Heat olive oil in a frying pan over high heat and seal the lamb for about 4 minutes on each side. Transfer to the oven and bake at 220°C for 7 minutes, then remove from the oven and allow to rest in a warm place for 5 minutes.

In a blender, process tomatoes and extra virgin olive oil until finely puréed. Heat tomato purée in a saucepan. In a separate saucepan, combine the artichoke purée, butter and cream and heat gently until the artichoke purée is warm.

To serve, slice the lamb, place on the artichoke purée and pour the tomato sauce around.

SERVES 4

anatra arrosto con polenta
ROAST DUCK WITH WET POLENTA

2 corn-fed ducks (size 17)
1 head garlic, cut in half
100 ml balsamic vinegar
800 ml Brown Chicken Stock (see page 153)
600 ml water
200 g medium-grain polenta
50 g parmesan cheese, grated

Put half a head of garlic into the cavity of each duck. Place ducks in a high-sided baking tray and sprinkle them with balsamic vinegar. Cover with aluminium foil and bake for 2 hours at 180°C, removing the foil for the last 30 minutes of cooking.

In a saucepan, bring chicken stock to the boil. Lower the heat and simmer until the stock is reduced to 400 ml.

In another saucepan, bring the water to the boil, rain the polenta into it, and stir continuously for 5 minutes. Remove from heat and allow to sit for 15 minutes.

Meanwhile, cut the ducks in half and remove all bones. Before serving, add grated parmesan cheese to polenta and pour the reduced chicken stock around each duck.

To serve, pile polenta onto serving plates and top each with half a duck.

SERVES 4

Bryan Westwood, Ceramic plate, 1998

ANATRA ARROSTO CON POLENTA >

bollito misto
MIXED BOILED MEATS WITH GREEN SAUCE AND MOSTARDA FRUITS

1 small veal tongue (approximately 400 g)
4 lamb shanks, frenched (ask your butcher to cut off some of the bone so that it will look neater when cooking)
8 chipolata sausages
10 cloves garlic, peeled
4 onions, peeled and roughly chopped
12 baby carrots, peeled
6 baby beetroots, peeled (in this recipe we want the beets to lose some colour)
12 baby turnips, peeled
1 cup Green Sauce (see page 159)
½ cup Mostarda fruits, chopped
Extra virgin olive oil

In three separate pots, boil the veal tongue, shanks and sausages with equal quantities of garlic and onions. Cook the tongue and shank for 1½ hours and the sausages for 30 minutes. Boil baby vegetables in salted water for 7 minutes.

To serve, slice tongue about ½ cm thick. Arrange the tongue and other meats on 4 serving plates. Separate the vegetables and arrange them attractively on the plates. Spoon salsa verde on top of meats, sprinkle with chopped Mostarda fruits and drizzle with extra virgin olive oil. (When assembling this dish, you have to work fairly quickly to ensure that everything remains hot.)

SERVES 4

NOTE Mostarda fruits are candied fruit which are marinated in mustard seed as well as a thick sugar syrup. The taste is sweet but hot and can be overpowering if too much is used. Mostarda fruits are available at any good delicatessen.

costoletta di vitello con peperoni gialli, ceci e parmigiano
GRILLED VEAL CUTLET WITH CHICKPEAS, YELLOW CAPSICUM AND PARMESAN

180 g dried chickpeas
6 cloves garlic, peeled
4 milk-fed veal cutlets (approximately 250 g each)
Olive oil for grilling
4 tblsp extra virgin olive oil
2 yellow capsicums, seeded and diced
60 g parmesan cheese, shaved

Before cooking chickpeas, soak in cold water for 12 hours, then drain chickpeas and discard soaking water. Place chickpeas and garlic in a pot and cover with water. Cook over medium heat for 1½ hours or until tender.

Brush veal cutlets with a little olive oil and grill on medium to high for about 8 minutes on each side. Remove veal from grill and allow to rest in a warm place for 5 minutes.

Gently heat extra virgin olive oil in a frying pan, add capsicums and cook until soft. Add drained chickpeas and heat through. Before serving, mix shaved parmesan with chickpeas and capsicum.

To serve, arrange chickpeas on serving plates then top with veal.

SERVES 4

< BOLLITO MISTO

COSTOLETTA DI VITELLO CON PEPERONI GIALLI, CECI E PARMIGIANO

costoletta di vitello con zucchine, spec e bocconcini
VEAL CUTLET WITH ZUCCHINI, SPECK AND BOCCONCINI

150 ml extra virgin olive oil
4 milk-fed veal cutlets (approximately 250 g each)
1 onion, peeled and diced
250 g speck, diced
2 large zucchini, finely sliced
6 bocconcini of mozzarella, diced

Heat 50 ml of the olive oil in a frying pan over high heat and seal cutlets for 5–6 minutes on each side. Transfer them to the oven and bake at 200°C for 15 minutes. Remove from the oven and allow to rest in a warm place for 5 minutes.

In a frying pan, gently heat the remaining olive oil, and cook onion and speck for 3 minutes, then add zucchini and cook for a further 2 minutes. Add the bocconcini, mix quickly and remove from heat.

To serve, arrange the zucchini mixture on individual plates with the veal slightly overlapping.

SERVES 4

cotechino con lenticchie
GRILLED COTECHINO WITH LENTILS

2 cotechino sausages (approximately 400 g each)
240 g du Puy lentils
400 ml White Chicken Stock (see page 153)

Before cooking, prick the cotechino with a fork several times. In a large pot, cover cotechino with water and bring to the boil over high heat. Reduce the heat and simmer for 2 hours. Change the water twice during these 2 hours of cooking, each time bringing the water to the boil then reducing the heat to a simmer. When cotechino is ready, allow to cool then peel.

In a large saucepan, combine lentils and chicken stock and bring to the boil over high heat. Reduce heat and simmer for 20 minutes, stirring occasionally. The lentils should have soaked up almost all the chicken stock.

Slice cotechino and grill or fry on high for 2 minutes on each side.

To serve, arrange cotechino slices evenly on four plates and pour the lentils around.

SERVES 4

NOTE Du Puy lentils are a French lentil and can be cooked without prior soaking. They also tend to hold their shape better than normal lentils. If du Puy lentils are unavailable, normal brown lentils will do, but remember to soak them before cooking and that they may take a little longer to cook.

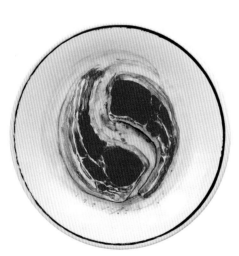

Tim Storrier, Ceramic plate, 1998

fegato alla cipolla fondente
GRILLED CALVES' LIVER WITH MELTED ONIONS

Tim Storrier, *Point to Point*
(The Midday Blaze Line),
1992, acrylic on canvas

100 g butter
6 large onions, peeled and sliced
6 bay leaves
720 g cleaned calves' liver (ask the butcher to clean and slice it for you)
Olive oil for cooking
Fresh chervil, chopped (optional)

Melt the butter in a large saucepan. Add onions and bay leaves and cook over low
heat, covered, for 30 minutes, stirring occasionally. Brush the liver with a little olive oil
and grill on high or fry for about 2 minutes on each side. The veal liver is cooked when
beads of blood appear on the surface once it has been turned over.

To serve, spread the melted onions on 4 plates, top with the liver and garnish with a
little chervil if desired.

SERVES 4

fegato di vitello con salsa di olive verdi
GRILLED VEAL LIVER WITH PANCETTA AND GREEN OLIVE SALSA

120 g (½ cup) green olives, pitted
8 French eschallots, peeled
1 clove garlic, peeled
1 tblsp salt-packed capers, washed under
   running water for 5 minutes
80 ml extra virgin olive oil

30 g butter
120 g pancetta, chopped
720 g veal liver (ask the butcher to clean
   and slice it for you)
Olive oil for grilling

In a blender, combine olives, eschallots, garlic, capers and extra virgin olive oil. Purée for
2 minutes (the salsa should not be too fine). Melt butter in a pan, add pancetta and
cook for 5 minutes on low heat. Set aside.

Brush the liver with a little olive oil and grill on high for about 2 minutes on each side.
The veal liver is cooked when beads of blood appear on the surface once it has been
turned over.

To serve, arrange the liver on top of the olive salsa. Sprinkle the pancetta all over and
drizzle with a little of the cooking juices.

SERVES 4

filetto di vitello con polenta e salsa alla pizzaiola
ROAST VEAL FILLET WITH POLENTA, DICED TOMATOES, OREGANO AND CAPERS

Polenta (see page 157)
Olive oil for cooking
800 g veal fillet, cleaned
100 ml extra virgin olive oil
4 tomatoes, peeled, seeded and diced
2 tsp fresh oregano, chopped
2 tblsp salt-packed capers, washed under running water for 5 minutes

Prepare polenta. When cooked, spread in a tray to a thickness of about 2–3 cm. When cool, cut into 4 circles approximately 6 cm in diameter.

Using a boning knife, remove any silver skin and excess fat from the veal fillet. In a large pan, heat olive oil over high heat and seal veal fillet for about 4 minutes on each side. Transfer to the oven and cook at 220°C for 9 minutes. Remove from oven and allow to rest for 5 minutes in a warm place.

While the veal is resting, gently heat extra virgin olive oil in a saucepan, add tomatoes, oregano and capers and cook for 3 minutes. Bake polenta in the hot oven for 2 minutes to warm it slightly.

To serve, slice veal, place on top of polenta and arrange diced tomatoes, capers and oregano around.

SERVES 4

Ken Johnson, red wine label
'Rosso di Luni'

filetto di manzo alle erbe
HERB-GRILLED BEEF TENDERLOIN ON CELERIAC WITH TOMATO AND LEMON JUICE

160 g celeriac, peeled
Juice of 1 lemon
2 tomatoes, peeled, seeded and diced
4 tblsp extra virgin olive oil
800 g beef fillet, cleaned
2 tsp fresh tarragon
2 tsp fresh chervil
2 tsp fresh basil
2 tsp fresh thyme
2 tsp fresh parsley
Olive oil for grilling

Cut celeriac into strips 2 mm wide by 4 cm long. Toss them in lemon juice straight away to stop the celeriac from discolouring. Add tomatoes and extra virgin olive oil, toss well and set aside.

Using a boning knife, remove any silver skin and excess fat from the beef fillet. Cut beef into 4 even steaks. Combine all the herbs, chop them, and roll the beef in the mixed chopped herbs. Grill the steaks on medium to high with a little olive oil for 8 minutes on each side. Once cooked, allow to rest in a warm place for 5 minutes, then serve on celeriac.

SERVES 4

< FILETTO DI VITELLO CON POLENTA
E SALSA ALLA PIZZAIOLA

filetto di manzo con porri e pesto
GRILLED BEEF FILLET WITH BRAISED LEEKS AND PESTO

50 g butter
4 leeks (white parts only), cleaned and julienned
150 ml White Chicken Stock (see page 153)
800 g beef fillet, cleaned
Olive oil for grilling
4 tblsp Pesto (see page 156)

Melt butter in a large saucepan, add leeks and cook on low heat for 10 minutes. Add chicken stock and increase the heat a little. Cook for a further 10 minutes.

Using a boning knife, remove any silver skin and excess fat from the beef fillet. Cut beef into 4 even steaks. Grill on medium to high with a little olive oil for 8 minutes on each side. Once cooked, allow to rest in a warm place for 5 minutes. Serve on braised leeks with a tablespoon of pesto on each fillet.

SERVES 4

galletto disossato con pancetta e porcini
BONED SPATCHCOCK STUFFED WITH PANCETTA AND PORCINI MUSHROOMS

4 spatchcocks (size 4)
½ cup dried porcini mushrooms
30 g butter
100 g pancetta, chopped
240 g pork mince
Olive oil for cooking

Ken Johnson, red wine label
'Niccolo V'

If you cannot bone spatchcocks, you should be able to purchase them pre-boned from any good poultry shop. (Ask them to leave the leg bones in and the wings on for presentation.)

Before using, soak porcini mushrooms in hot water for 30 minutes then drain them and discard the soaking water. Melt butter in a frying pan, add pancetta and porcini mushrooms and cook over low heat for 10 minutes. Once cooked, allow to cool, then mix with pork mince. Place pork mixture onto boned spatchcocks. Using a brightly coloured string, sew them up so they look like whole birds again. In a large frying pan, heat the olive oil over high heat and seal the stuffed birds all over. This will take about 6–7 minutes. Transfer to the oven and roast at 180°C for 30 minutes. When cooked, allow to rest for 5 minutes, then remove the string and serve the birds with the pan juices.

SERVES 4

NOTE In this recipe we use brightly coloured cotton string so that it is easy to find when the birds are cooked. Use jute or cotton string, not nylon or other types that will melt.

FILETTO DI MANZO CON PORRI E PESTO >

involtini di galletto disossato con frittata
INVOLTINI OF SPATCHCOCK FILLED WITH VEGETABLES ON FRITTATA

4 spatchcocks (size 4)
1 carrot, peeled
1 stick celery, peeled
1 leek (white part only), washed
30 g butter
½ bunch fresh thyme, chopped
Olive oil for cooking

FRITTATA
3 eggs
50 ml cream
1 tblsp parmesan cheese, grated

Deruta hand-painted convent
floor tile

If you cannot bone spatchcocks, you should be able to purchase them pre-boned from any good poultry shop. (There must be no bones at all.)

Cut all vegetables into strips 1 cm wide by 5 cm long. Melt butter in a frying pan, add the vegetables and thyme and cook for 6–7 minutes over low heat. When cooked, set aside to cool. Once vegetables are cold, arrange them lengthways on the 4 spatchcocks, then roll the birds over so they look like stuffed tubes. Once rolled, tie 3 pieces of string around each bird. In a large frying pan, heat olive oil over high heat and seal spatchcocks all over. This will take about 6–7 minutes. Transfer spatchcocks to the oven and roast at 180°C for 20 minutes. Once cooked, remove from pan and allow to rest for 5 minutes in a warm place, then slice in half on an angle.

TO MAKE FRITTATA In a bowl, mix eggs and cream with a fork. Add parmesan and pour into a small ovenproof frying pan. Bake at 180°C for 10 minutes, then remove from oven and allow to cool.

To serve, slice the frittata like a cake into 8 pieces. Place 2 slices on each plate and top with the involtini halves, cut side up. Drizzle with some of the cooking juices.

SERVES 4

medaglioni di vitello con salsa ai funghi di bosco
VEAL MEDALLIONS WRAPPED IN PANCETTA WITH WILD MUSHROOM SAUCE

Olive oil for cooking
¼ cup dried porcini mushrooms
4 shiitake mushrooms, sliced
4 slippery jack mushrooms, sliced
2 milk-cap mushrooms, sliced

200 ml Brown Chicken Stock (see page 153)
200 ml Brown Veal Stock (see page 153)
800 g veal fillet, cleaned
8 thin slices pancetta

Before using, soak porcini mushrooms in boiling water for 30 minutes, then drain, discard soaking water and slice mushrooms. In a large saucepan, heat a little olive oil, add all the mushrooms and cook over medium heat for 10 minutes. Add both stocks and bring to the boil, then reduce heat and simmer for 20 minutes.

Using a boning knife, remove any silver skin and excess fat from the veal fillet. Cut the veal into 8 even medallions and wrap 1 slice of pancetta around each. Heat some more olive oil in a large frying pan and seal the medallions on both sides over high heat for 4 minutes on each side. Transfer to the oven and cook at 220°C for 6 minutes. Remove from the oven and allow to rest for 5 minutes in a warm place. Serve with wild mushroom sauce.

SERVES 4

< INVOLTINI DI GALLETTO
DISOSSATO CON FRITTATA

quaglie alla salvia
QUAILS WITH CRISPY SAGE, EGGPLANT AND FRESH TOMATOES

8 medium quails (approximately 150 g each)
4 longton eggplants (these are long, skinny eggplants)
Salt
Olive oil for cooking
1 bunch fresh sage
6 vine-ripened tomatoes, peeled, seeded and diced
80 ml extra virgin olive oil

Cut the backbones out of the quails so that they will lie flat. Set aside.

Cut eggplants in half lengthways and sprinkle with a generous amount of salt. Leave for 15 minutes to allow the bitter juices to drain, then wash eggplants and pat dry with a paper towel. Drizzle olive oil over eggplants and bake at 220°C for 10 minutes.

While the eggplants are cooking, heat a generous amount of olive oil in a small saucepan over hight heat, add sage and leave to crisp up (2–3 minutes). Remove sage from oil and place on paper towel to drain.

Baste quails with some olive oil and grill on high for 4 minutes on each side. Gently heat extra virgin olive oil in a medium saucepan, add the diced tomatoes and cook until just warmed through.

To serve, place tomatoes on 4 plates, criss-cross them with the eggplant and top with quails. Crush the crispy sage and sprinkle over.

SERVES 4

salsicce di coniglio su insalata di fave e parmigiano
RABBIT SAUSAGES WITH BROAD BEANS AND PARMESAN CHEESE

1 kg wild rabbit meat (approximately 2 rabbits)
200 g prosciutto
100 g back fat (from a pig)
½ bunch fresh parsley, chopped
60 ml (2 nips) dry sherry

8 x 12-cm-length sausage skin
Olive oil for cooking
100 g broad beans, shelled
80 g parmesan cheese, shaved
4 tblsp Lemon Juice Olive Oil (see page 156)

Process rabbit meat, prosciutto and back fat through a mincer. In a large bowl, combine mince with parsley and sherry and mix well. Pipe the mixture into sausage skin, allowing some waste, and tie or twist sausage every 12 cm to make 8 sausages. Boil sausages for 2 minutes then refresh under cold water immediately. When cold, cut and peel the skins off the sausages. Place skinless sausages in a tray with a little olive oil and bake at 180°C for 10–15 minutes.

While the sausages are cooking, boil shelled broad beans for 3 minutes. Drain and mix in a bowl with shaved parmesan and lemon juice olive oil.

To serve, place sausages on top of broad bean salad.

SERVES 4

< Making sausages

Ken Johnson, *Diagonal*, 1998, oil on canvas

vitello tonnato
COLD VEAL WITH FRESH TUNA MAYONNAISE

800 g veal fillet, cleaned
Olive oil for cooking
1 cup Fresh Tuna Mayonnaise (see page 154)
Capers (optional)
Black olives, chopped (optional)

Using a boning knife, remove any silver skin and excess fat from the veal fillet. In a large frying pan, heat olive oil over high heat and seal veal on both sides. Transfer to the oven and cook at 220°C for 9 minutes. Remove from pan and cool on a wire rack for 20–30 minutes or until at room temperature.

To serve, place 2 tablespoons of mayonnaise on each of 4 plates. Slice veal and arrange on top of mayonnaise, then spoon the rest of the mayonnaise over. Sprinkle with some capers and chopped black olives if desired.

SERVES 4

zampone ripieno di lenticchie e spinaci
STUFFED PIGS' HOCKS WITH ENGLISH SPINACH AND LENTILS

4 pigs' hocks
2 onions, chopped
2 carrots, chopped
1 stick celery, chopped
750 ml Brown Veal Stock (see page 153)
240 g du Puy lentils

400 ml White Chicken Stock (see page 153)
250 g chicken mince
2 tsp fresh thyme, chopped
2 bunches fresh English spinach, blanched

Scrape pigs' hocks with a knife and remove the bone. Place in a medium-sized roasting pan with onions, carrots, celery and veal stock. Cover with aluminium foil and bake at 180°C for 2 hours.

In a large saucepan, combine lentils and chicken stock over high heat, bring to the boil then reduce heat and simmer for 20 minutes, stirring occasionally.

Remove hocks from pan and scrape meat and fat from the hock skins. Chop the meat and half the fat, then mix with chicken mince and thyme. Place filling on hock skins, roll skins up and wrap in aluminium foil, turning the ends so they look like bon bons. Bake at 180°C for 20 minutes, then remove from foil and cut each hock in half.

To serve, arrange the hocks on top of the spinach, and surround with lentils.

SERVES 4

NOTE Du Puy lentils are a French lentil and can be cooked without prior soaking. They also tend to hold their shape better than normal lentils. If du Puy lentils are unavailable, normal brown lentils will do, but remember to soak them before cooking and that they may take a little longer to cook.

ABOVE: Tim Storrier,
Mothers Garden II, 1990,
acrylic on panel

OPPOSITE: Tim Storrier,
Reef Dreaming II, 1990,
acrylic on panel

for Lucio   Lanceley 99

insalate e contorni

Edmond's Tomato Salad

This is a salad that encompasses enduring friendship, geography and great food. In our household it is always something special.

I was taught to make it in the village of Mojácar in southern Spain by a Sephardic Jew from Fez — the Moroccan novelist Edmond Elmaleh. His wife, Marie Cecile, is *une femme intellectuelle* — a biographer of the philosopher and literary critic Walter Benjamin. At the time of the French Revolution her family, members of the haute bourgeoisie, purchased the monastery of Lugny in Burgundy with all its supporting farmlands.

This French–Moroccan family adopted my family, so this recipe has made a journey of friendship from Mojácar, where we first met, to an apartment in Boulevard du Montparnasse where Edmond and Marie Cecile live, and to the Moulin — part of the monastery in Burgundy still owned by Marie Cecile's family — where we have spent many European summers and snow-covered Christmases with our French family, who gather there en masse at holiday times.

This salad has also accompanied me on an artistic journey. In paintings and drawings I have used images from the very North African landscape of Andalusia, where we stayed in a cubist hill town of Moorish origins, from the shores of the Mediterranean and from Burgundy — most notably from the caves, fields and vineyards of the road to Chablis.

Of all salads, this one is for me the most memorable and is laden with associations with the best of people and the best of places. It has been a closely guarded secret in our family until now.

I give it away only for Lucio and Sally.

You will need about 2 kilograms of tomatoes for 8 people. It is essential that you find really good ripe tomatoes, which can be a challenge. Marmande or Ox-heart varieties, the knobbly ones, are best, and they must be deep, luminous red — red all the way through. Don't use those insipid pink ones. Allow at least a couple of tomatoes per person, depending on size. Quarter each one and slice the quarters across into 2 or 3 pieces.

Put the tomatoes into a largish bowl, then add 3 or 4 cloves of garlic, finely chopped, and a good handful each of finely chopped parsley and fresh coriander leaves.

Finely grind and add 2 tablespoons of coriander seeds, 1 tablespoon of cumin seeds and 4 dried birdseye chillies.

Then add 1 tablespoon of paprika, 1 teaspoon of salt, 1 tablespoon of preserved lemon, finely diced, and finally about a cup of the best olive oil.

Mix all together gently with your hands, allow to stand for about an hour, then eat.

Wonderful on its own with good crusty bread; great with lamb brochettes or any grilled or barbecued meat.

If there is any left over — a rare occurrence — it can be cooked and sieved to make a good spicy tomato sauce.

PAGE 134 Colin Lanceley, *Edmond's Salad*, 1999, crayon on paper

COLIN LANCELEY

asparagi e noci
ASPARAGUS AND WALNUTS

4 tblsp walnut kernels
3 bunches asparagus
120 ml Salad Dressing (see page 150)

Place walnuts on a baking tray and bake at 180°C for 10 minutes. Place the hot nuts in a teatowel and rub to remove skins from the nuts. Discard the tough end of the asparagus and boil the stalks in salted water for 3–4 minutes (depending on their thickness). Cut asparagus in half, dress with walnuts and salad dressing and serve immediately.

SERVES 4

NOTE This can also be served as a cold salad.

Colin Lanceley, *Sculpture and Model*, 1994, mixed media

fave e pecorino
BROAD BEANS AND SHAVED PECORINO CHEESE

600 g young, tender broad beans, unshelled
3 tomatoes, seeded and diced
180 g imported soft Pecorino cheese, shaved
120 ml extra virgin olive oil
Rock salt, crushed, to taste

For this recipe you must use only the very smallest and youngest broad beans possible.

Shell the beans and place them in a bowl. Toss beans together with all the other ingredients. Season with crushed rock salt and serve immediately.

SERVES 6

insalata di rucola, peperoni e caprino
ROCKET, ROAST CAPSICUM AND GOAT'S CHEESE SALAD

6 red Roast Capsicums (see page 34)
3 punnets baby rocket
150 ml Salad Dressing (see page 150)
1 log Kryton goat's cheese, sliced into 5-mm discs

Cut roasted capsicum into long strips. Wash and dry rocket and combine in a large bowl with the capsicum, salad dressing and slices of goat's cheese.

SERVES 6

NOTE If Kryton goat's cheese is unavailable, any good quality mild, creamy goat's cheese will do.

FAVE E PECORINO; INSALATA CAPRESE CLASSICA; INSALATA DI RADICCHIO, RUCOLA E FINOCCHIO >

insalata caprese classica

TOMATO, BOCCONCINI AND BASIL SALAD

9 vine-ripened tomatoes
6 fresh bocconcini of mozzarella, sliced
12 fresh basil leaves, very finely sliced
Extra virgin olive oil

Slice tomatoes crossways as thinly as possible. Spread them evenly on a large platter, place bocconcini slices on top and sprinkle sliced basil all over. Drizzle with extra virgin olive oil.

SERVES 6

Fred Cress, *Lunch 1*, 1991, pastel and ink on paper

Fred Cress, *Lunch 2*, 1991, pastel and ink on paper

insalata di carciofi e parmigiano
SALAD OF RAW ARTICHOKES AND PARMESAN CHEESE

12 small globe artichokes, with their stalks
Juice of 2 lemons
Extra virgin olive oil to taste
180 g Reggiano parmesan cheese, shaved

Peel the artichokes, leaving only the pale centre. Cut artichokes in half from tip to
stalk. If the choke is at all prickly, remove it with a spoon. With a sharp knife, slice the
artichokes very finely. Toss in a bowl with lemon juice, some extra virgin olive oil and half
the parmesan. Top with the remaining cheese and serve.

SERVES 6

insalata di fichi e rughetta
GREEN FIG AND BABY ROCKET SALAD

15 small ripe green figs
3 punnets of baby rocket
120 ml Lemon Juice Olive Oil (see page 156)
Extra virgin olive oil

Slice figs crossways as thinly as possible. Fan the figs in a single line around the edge of a large platter. Wash and dry the rocket. Mix rocket in a large bowl with lemon juice olive oil. Place rocket in the centre of the platter. Drizzle extra virgin olive oil over the figs and serve immediately.

SERVES 6

insalata di pere, rucola e parmigiano
PEAR, ROCKET AND PARMESAN SALAD

6 firm pears
Juice of 2 lemons
3 punnets baby rocket
180 g parmesan cheese, shaved
Extra virgin olive oil

Peel and quarter the pears, removing the seeds and stalks. Slice pears thinly and arrange around the edge of a large platter. Drizzle with lemon juice to prevent them from discolouring. Wash and dry the rocket and combine in a large bowl with the cheese. Drizzle rocket with olive oil, toss well, and serve in the centre of the sliced pears.

SERVES 6

insalata di radicchio, rucola e finocchio
ROCKET, RADICCHIO AND FENNEL SALAD

2 heads fennel
1 head red-leaf radicchio
2 punnets baby rocket
120 ml Lemon Juice Olive Oil (see page 156)

Wash and trim fennel and slice very thinly. Remove the outer leaves of the radicchio, leaving only the heart. Wash well and slice into very fine strips. Wash and dry the rocket. Place fennel and all leaves in a large bowl, toss with lemon juice olive oil and serve immediately.

OPPOSITE: Massimo Giannoni, *Landscape near Mudgee*, 1994, oil on canvas

SERVES 4

Ken Johnson, *Re-route*, 1993, oil on canvas

insalata tricolore
WITLOF, ROCKET AND RADICCHIO SALAD

2 punnets rocket
1 head red-leaf radicchio
2 heads witlof
120 ml Lemon Juice Olive Oil (see page 156)

Wash and dry the rocket and radicchio. Remove outer leaves of radicchio, leaving only the heart, and slice into thin strips. Slice witlof crossways very finely. In a large bowl, mix all the leaves with the lemon juice olive oil. Serve immediately.

SERVES 4

patate novelle arrosto
ROSEMARY-ROASTED POTATOES

400 g new potatoes
100 ml olive oil
50 g butter
½ bunch (12 sprigs) fresh rosemary, chopped

Place potatoes in a pot, cover with water, bring to the boil, then drain. Heat olive oil and butter in a baking tray, add potatoes and rosemary, and bake at 220°C for 15–20 minutes or until golden brown. Serve immediately.

SERVES 4

spinaci e pinoli
SPINACH AND PINENUTS

4 tbls pinenuts
4 bunches fresh English spinach
120 ml Lemon Juice Olive Oil (see page 156)

Place pinenuts on a baking tray and roast at 180°C for 10 minutes or until golden brown. Wash spinach and boil in salted water for 2 minutes. Strain spinach and squeeze out the excess water. Place in a serving bowl, dress with lemon juice olive oil and sprinkle pinenuts over.

SERVES 4

salse e condimenti

Recipe for a Great Restaurant

INGREDIENTS

LOCATION Secluded tree-lined boulevard in a fashionable inner suburb.

DECOR Tastefully furnished and decorated with works by Australia's leading artists. Can be changed by simply re-hanging artworks.

MENU Beautifully illustrated by Australia's pre-eminent landscape artist. Large variety of dishes so confusing to most clients that they order the daily special or Green Tagliolini with Blue Swimmer Crab.

WINE LIST Illustrated by Australia's leading artist–wine connoisseur, to create a feeling of thirst and such fascination with the drawings that one ignores the prices.

RESTAURATEUR Possessing a genuine love for people, for food and for drink.
Possessing an even greater love for people who eat and drink.
Possessing an absolute passion for people who eat and drink in his restaurant.
Having a genuine smile for even the most unwelcome drunk patron.
Retaining a sense of humour even when his accountant arrives unannounced from Melbourne, and the restaurant is completely booked out.
Has eyes in the back of his head, to see who needs something before that person realises it.
Has a well-rounded personality, preferable with a well-rounded figure, which gives patrons a feeling of comfort, knowing that the food offered has been thoroughly researched.

CLIENTELE Cultivate impoverished artists, accountants and other interesting patrons.
Occasionally allow successful business people, politicians, premiers, ex-prime
ministers and celebrities to mingle with the regulars.

STAFF Ensure that waiters always wear interesting ties; it creates a wonderful topic
of conversation if one's guests are not very interesting.

Ensure that waiters retain a sense of humour and apologise to guests for the
bad weather, the political uncertainties, unemployment and whatever else is
of concern.

Develop the Italian accent, even if the waiters are Spanish or Hungarian.

INSTRUCTIONS In order to achieve a successful result, mix the above ingredients and
ensure that you heed the following golden rules to success.

Don't listen to your accountant.

Listen to your accountant's wife. 'Don't use too much oil.'

Ignore the profit motive.

Ignore suggested profit mark-ups on wines.

Always buy the best-quality ingredients, irrespective of price, even though you
know that very few will know the difference.

Be generous to clients that you like. Offer them complimentary bottles of
champagne, wine or cognac.

You may not make much money, but you will continue to be the most successful
and best-loved restaurateur.

Salute Lucio!

From your equally well-rounded friends,

SYLVIA AND TOM LOWENSTEIN

condimento per insalata
SALAD DRESSING

12 French eschallots, finely diced
6 cloves garlic, peeled and sliced
150 ml white wine vinegar
Salt and pepper to taste
375 ml extra virgin olive oil

In a bowl, mix shallots, garlic, vinegar, salt and pepper. While whisking constantly, gently pour olive oil into the vinegar. Allow to rest for at least one hour.

condimento piccante
PIQUANT SAUCE

50 ml extra virgin olive oil
6 cloves garlic, finely chopped
2 carrots, peeled and finely diced
1 tblsp chopped chillies
3 large ripe tomatoes, peeled, seeded and diced
3 tblsp white sugar
1 tblsp red wine vinegar

In a large saucepan, heat the olive oil and sweat the garlic and carrots over low heat for about 3 minutes. Add chillies, tomatoes, sugar and vinegar and cook for a further 10 minutes. Add salt and pepper.

NOTE Let the sauce cool and place in an air-tight container. It will keep for up to 1 week in the refrigerator.

OPPOSITE: Mark Schaller, *Glass and Bottle*, 1998, oil on canvas

BELOW: Carlo Montesi, *Study for La Cantoria*, 1994, mixed media on paper

condimento appetitoso
MIXED CAPSICUM AND RED WINE VINEGAR CONDIMENT

2 red capsicums
2 yellow capsicums
2 green capsicums
1 Spanish onion, peeled and diced very finely
50 g black olives, pitted and chopped
50 g whole baby capers
50 g small gherkins, chopped
2 tblsp red wine vinegar
Extra virgin olive oil (enough to cover)

Seed the capsicums and dice very finely. Mix all ingredients together in a large bowl. Cover with the olive oil and allow to stand for 2–3 hours.

NOTE Place condiment in an air-tight container. It will keep for up to 2 weeks in the refrigerator.

George Raftopoulos, *Untitled*,
1998, oil on canvas

fondo bianco di vitello
WHITE VEAL STOCK

10 kg veal bones
2 onions, peeled and chopped
2 carrots, peeled and chopped

3 sticks celery, chopped
1 head garlic, cut in half
1 bunch fresh thyme

Place veal bones, vegetables, garlic and thyme in a large pot. Cover with hot water and bring to the boil. Reduce the heat and simmer for 4–6 hours, skimming away any impurities that may rise to the surface. Strain and allow to cool.

fondo bianco di pollo
WHITE CHICKEN STOCK

10 kg chicken bones
2 onions, peeled and chopped
2 carrots, peeled and chopped

3 sticks celery, chopped
1 head garlic, cut in half
1 bunch fresh thyme

Place chicken bones, vegetables, garlic and thyme in a large pot. Cover with hot water and bring to the boil. Reduce the heat and simmer for 3–4 hours, skimming away any impurities that may rise to the surface. Strain and allow to cool.

David van Nunen, *Mask*, 1997

fondo bruno di pollo
BROWN CHICKEN STOCK

10 kg chicken bones
2 onions, peeled and chopped
2 carrots, peeled and chopped

3 sticks celery, chopped
1 head garlic, cut in half
1 bunch fresh thyme

Place all ingredients in a roasting pan and bake for 30 minutes at 200°C. Transfer to a large pot. Cover with hot water and bring to the boil. Reduce the heat and simmer for 3–4 hours, skimming away any impurities that may rise to the surface. Strain and allow to cool.

fondo bruno di vitello
BROWN VEAL STOCK

10 kg veal bones
2 onions, peeled and chopped
2 carrots, peeled and chopped

3 sticks celery, chopped
1 head garlic, cut in half
1 bunch fresh thyme

Place all ingredients in a roasting pan and bake for 30 minutes at 200°C. Transfer to a large pot. Cover with hot water and bring to the boil. Reduce the heat and simmer for 4–6 hours, skimming away any impurities that may rise to the surface. Strain and allow to cool.

fumetto di pesce
FISH STOCK

100 ml olive oil
5 kg snapper or red emperor bones
2 onions, peeled and chopped
3 sticks celery, chopped
2 leeks, washed and chopped
1 head garlic, cut in half
1 bunch fresh thyme

Place olive oil, fish bones, vegetables, garlic and thyme in a large pot. Cook over low heat for 10 minutes. Cover with cold water. Turn heat up to high and bring to the boil. Reduce heat and simmer for 20–30 minutes, skimming away any impurities that may rise to the surface. Strain and allow to cool.

maionese al tonno fresco
FRESH TUNA MAYONNAISE

2 whole eggs
4 egg yolks
2 tsp Dijon mustard
Juice of 1 lemon
400 ml olive oil

200 g fresh tuna, grilled and chopped
20 g anchovies, chopped
60 ml sherry vinegar
Salt and pepper to taste
3 tblsp natural yoghurt

Whisk whole eggs, yolks, mustard and lemon juice in a large bowl until combined. Slowly pour a thin stream of olive oil into the egg mixture, whisking vigorously until all oil is incorporated. Add tuna, anchovies, vinegar, salt and pepper, then fold in yoghurt.

NOTE This is our sauce for the Cold Veal with Fresh Tuna Mayonnaise (see page 133).

maionese classica
CLASSIC MAYONNAISE

2 whole eggs
4 egg yolks
2 tsp Dijon mustard
Juice of 1 lemon

400 ml olive oil
60 ml sherry vinegar
Salt and pepper to taste
3 tblsp natural yoghurt

Whisk whole eggs, yolks, mustard and lemon juice in a large bowl until combined. Slowly pour a thin stream of olive oil into the egg mixture, whisking vigorously until all oil is incorporated. Add vinegar, salt and pepper, then fold in yoghurt.

NOTE Place mayonnaise in an air-tight container. It will keep for up to 1 week in the refrigerator.

John Beard, Ceramic plate, 1998

Fred Cress, *Garden of Some
Vanities*, 1996, acrylic on canvas

olio al basilico
BASIL DRESSING

1 bunch fresh basil
3 tblsp red wine vinegar
400 ml extra virgin olive oil
Salt and pepper to taste

In a blender, process basil and vinegar until smooth. (Be careful not to blend them for too long, as the friction will cause the basil to discolour.) Add olive oil, salt and pepper.

olio al limone
LEMON JUICE OLIVE OIL

6 lemons
550 ml extra virgin olive oil
Salt and pepper to taste

Juice the lemons into a bowl. Add the olive oil, salt and pepper and gently whisk for 1 minute before using.

olio al rosmarino
ROSEMARY-SCENTED OIL

1-litre bottle extra virgin olive oil
2 stalks fresh rosemary
1 whole clove garlic, unpeeled
1 red-hot chilli

Remove a little oil from the bottle. Place rosemary, garlic and chilli into the bottle and allow to stand for at least 3 days.

Serve with fresh bread.

NOTE Rosemary-scented oil is not suitable for use as a salad dressing because the flavour is too strong.

pesto
PESTO

2 bunches fresh basil (preferably with
    small leaves)
1 clove garlic
100 ml olive oil

80 g (½ cup) pinenuts, roasted
100 g (1 cup) parmesan cheese, finely
    grated

In a blender, process the basil, garlic and olive oil for about 60 seconds. Add the roasted pinenuts and blend until they are finely ground. Using the pulse button, add the parmesan. Pour into a sterilised glass jar and cover with a thin film of oil to stop the pesto from discolouring.

Jan Senbergs, Pen drawing
done at the table, 1991

Donald Friend, *Hill End*, 1948, watercolour on paper

polenta
POLENTA

1 ltr water
1 tsp sea salt
175 g medium-grain polenta flour

In a medium saucepan, bring water to the boil, then add the sea salt. Reduce the heat
to a simmer. Rain the polenta flour into the water, stirring with a whisk until completely
blended. It will then start to bubble vigorously. Reduce heat to low and cook the polenta
for 20–30 minutes, stirring from time to time to prevent it from catching on the bottom
of the pot. The polenta is cooked when it falls away from the sides of the saucepan.

When cooked, spread the hot polenta into a tray to a thickness of 2–3 cm. Allow to
cool, then cut into strips.

pomodori essicati al forno
OVEN-DRIED TOMATOES

Roma tomatoes
Sea salt
Extra virgin olive oil
Fresh oregano
Garlic

Slice Roma tomatoes in half lengthways, place on a tray and sprinkle with sea salt. Cook in a 50°C oven for 6–8 hours. Marinate tomatoes in olive oil, oregano and garlic and allow to stand for 1 hour before using.

NOTE If the tomatoes are completely covered with olive oil, they will keep for up to 1 month in the refrigerator.

Timothy Fisher and Harley
taking a break

pomodori essicati al sole
SUN-DRIED TOMATOES

Bell tomatoes
Sea salt
Extra virgin olive oil
Garlic (optional)
Fresh basil (optional)
Chillies (optional)

Slice bell tomatoes in half lengthways and remove seeds. Place tomatoes on trays and sprinkle with sea salt. Allow to dry slowly in the sun for a few days, bringing them inside at every sunset. Once one side has dried, turn the tomatoes over and repeat the procedure.

When the tomatoes are dry, place them in a sterilised glass jar and cover with olive oil. If desired, add garlic, basil and whole chillies.

salsa semplice di pomodoro
TOMATO SAUCE

150 g butter
3 onions, peeled and very finely chopped
6 500-g tins whole peeled tomatoes
4 tblsp white sugar

In a large pot, melt butter and cook onions over low heat for 10 minutes without allowing them to colour. Add the tomatoes, bring to the boil, then reduce the heat and simmer for 1½ hours. Add sugar and process through a food mill.

NOTE The sauce can be stored in an air-tight container in the refrigerator for 3 days.

salsa verde
GREEN SAUCE

½ bunch fresh curly parsley
1 tblsp gherkins
2 tblsp baby capers
1 tblsp anchovies

6 cloves garlic, blanched
100 ml extra virgin olive oil
3 tblsp red wine vinegar

Finely chop all ingredients separately, then mix together with olive oil and vinegar.

NOTE Place sauce in a glass jar. It will keep for up to 1 week in the refrigerator.

John Olsen, *Old Boots
Leisurely Humming*,
1993, oil on canvas

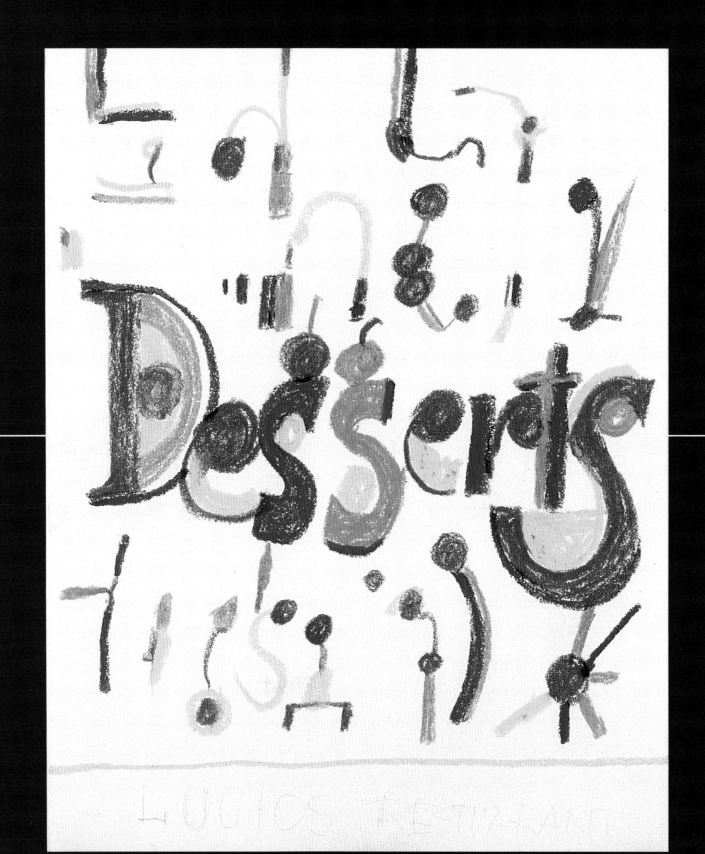

dolci

Lucio Prince of Provender:
the Man or the Food?

Is it the man or is it the food? Many have pondered but only those who frequent Lucio's temple of gastronomic delights will know: it is both. Like crabmeat and tagliolini, snapper and rock salt, gamberi and fagioli, they are indivisible, inextricably blended, a fusion; a most perfect unity of Renaissance man, our host, and impeccable cuisine known to the masticating classes of our shimmering seaside town.

Some could argue that in proper order face-filling comes first, the role of the culinary Sage mere subordinate to the salivating act, but they would be wrong. Lucio the man comes first, his impeccable fodder a marginal second, for the simple reason that Lucio is consummate, intrinsic, irreplaceable. Gustation is a time-honoured ritual and the spectre of barren lunchtimes, void of Lucio's tender ministrations to our highly attuned oral receptors and world-worn egos, would drive us to the abyss of despair; even, as some have had the effrontery to suggest, down the road to the competition.

It is well known to all who are artists, as equally to all who are not, that the art world is the most egoistical and disunited societal sub-group known to mankind except in one respect: its unanimous adulation of the undisputed champion of nosh. Similar affection for Lucio has been ascribed to the business world, from whose perturbed ranks certain 'notables' have been observed in varied states of advanced post-prandial thrall at the famed hostelry, a regard diminished by their dominant propensity: the primal love of profit margins above the loftier pleasures of sight and taste. Yet their presence is tolerated, even welcomed, for reasons only fully understood by the burgeoning congregation of lunchtime artists. They who alone recoil from the prospect of anything less than the altruistic conversion of the fiscally overburdened to the finer things of life; namely their own paintings, which liberally festoon Lucio's artfully ochred walls.

Since the late eighteenth century when a number of French hotels began boasting a table d'hôte there have been legions of restaurateurs of style, some verging on genius. Excelling is known to be a hard act and it hasn't become easier in our own time. Especially in Sydney, now renowned as the latest great Mecca of the gastronomic world, where names such as Armando, Gay, Tetsu, Tony and Attilio have become legend. So, how in such august company, then, does Lucio maintain his pre-eminence? Many say it's his personal way of welcoming you, because he makes you feel like invited guests at his own home. Some say it's because he grew up in his family's appositely named restaurant, Capannina Ciccio in Bocca di Magra. Others say it's because he still wears the tiepin that his kids gave him for his birthday. For my own modest part I know it is because he is special, a genuinely gracious man, engaged and engaging, one who possesses truly exceptional social and professional flair which he devotes unstintingly to the cause of our unhampered enjoyment.

WILLIAM WRIGHT

pasta dolce
SHORT SWEET PASTRY

500 g (4 cups) plain flour
75 g almond meal
75 g caster sugar

15 g salt
375 g unsalted butter, diced
3 whole eggs

On a clean, cold workbench, rub flour, almond meal, sugar, salt and butter together until all the butter is incorporated into the dry ingredients. Add eggs and mix together gently by hand to make a ball. Wrap in cling film then refrigerate for 30 minutes before using.

pasta salata
SHORT SAVOURY PASTRY

500 g (4 cups) plain flour
5 g salt

300 g unsalted butter, diced
4 whole eggs

On a clean, cold workbench, rub flour, salt and butter together until all the butter is incorporated into the dry ingredients. Add eggs and mix together gently by hand to make a ball. Wrap in cling film then refrigerate for 30 minutes before using.

bavarese con biscottini al brandy
BUTTERMILK BAVAROIS WITH BRANDY SNAPS

BAVAROIS
4 gelatine leaves
150g caster sugar
1 vanilla bean, split
350 ml pure cream
400 ml buttermilk
Mixed berries to serve (optional)

SNAPS
20 g golden syrup
30 g butter
1 tblsp brown sugar
30 g plain flour
1 pinch ground ginger

Soften gelatine in a bowl of cold water for 20 minutes. Heat sugar, vanilla bean and 100 ml of the cream over low heat until the sugar has dissolved. Remove from heat, add gelatine leaves and stir until they dissolve. Strain mixture through a fine sieve. Quickly pour buttermilk into the mixture, stirring until combined, then leave until almost set. Whisk the remaining cream until firm, then gently fold into mixture. Spoon into 6 180-ml moulds and refrigerate for least 6 hours before serving.

To serve, unmould bavarois by dipping them in a bowl of hot water for about 5 seconds before inverting each onto a serving plate. They should slip straight out. Serve with brandy snaps and mixed berries if desired.

TO MAKE SNAPS Preheat oven to 175°C. Heat golden syrup, butter and sugar over low heat, stirring until sugar his dissolved. Add sieved dry ingredients and stir well. Place teaspoonfuls of the brandy snap mixture onto a well-greased tray, leaving at least 5 cm between each. Bake in pre-heated oven for 6–7 minutes. Remove from oven, allow to cool slightly, then roll each biscuit around the handle of a wooden spoon. (Makes 12 snaps.)

SERVES 6

ABOVE: Francesco Petrollo, Forged bronze, 1996

OPPOSITE: Angus McDonald, *I say, stay in there, I'm not going*, 1996, oil on canvas

Salvatore Zofrea,
Landscape with Figs, 1993,
oil and marble dust on paper

budino al cioccolato con gelato alla vaniglia
CHOCOLATE PUDDING WITH VANILLA ICE CREAM

40 ml water
320 g caster sugar
200 g hazelnut kernels
200 g dark chocolate, chopped
90 g butter
5 eggs, separated

150 ml sour cream
100 g plain flour
¾ tsp baking powder
¾ tsp salt
Vanilla Ice Cream (see page 171)

Preheat oven to 175°C. In a heavy-based saucepan, combine water and 90 g of the sugar. Bring to the boil and cook until the mixture becomes a golden colour. Add hazelnuts and mix well. Remove from saucepan and pour into a metal tray. Allow to cool completely. Chop finely and set aside.

Place chocolate and butter in a bowl and melt in the microwave or over a double boiler if you do not have a microwave. In a large bowl, whisk egg yolks with 115 g of the sugar for 5 minutes. Add the sour cream, flour, baking powder, salt, chopped nuts and melted chocolate mixture. Fold all ingredients together gently.

In a separate bowl, whisk egg whites until they start to peak. Rain the remaining 115 g of the sugar onto the egg whites and whisk until sugar has dissolved. At this stage the egg whites should have firm but smooth peaks. Fold them into the chocolate mixture and spoon into 8 greased 120-ml Dariole moulds. Place moulds on a tray, cover with aluminium foil and bake for 35 minutes at 175°C. Once cooked, leave to cool for 5 minutes then invert onto 8 plates and serve with vanilla ice cream.

SERVES 8

budino alle pere, grappa e uva sultanina
PEAR, CURRANT AND GRAPPA PUDDING

75 g (½ cup) currants
125 ml (½ cup) grappa
6 pears
50 g unsalted butter
90 g (⅓ cup) caster sugar
Zest of 1 lemon
Double cream to serve

TOPPING
120 g unsalted butter
90 g (⅓ cup) sugar
1 vanilla bean, seeds only
3 large eggs, separated
60 g (½ cup) plain flour
170 ml (⅔ cup) milk
4 tblsp grappa
Pinch of salt

Preheat oven to 175°C. In a small bowl, combine currants and grappa and allow to soak for about 20 minutes. Peel and core pears and cut into 1-cm slices. In a large frying pan, melt the butter over medium heat. Add pears and sugar and cook for about 10 minutes, stirring occasionally. Add currants, grappa and lemon zest. Remove from heat. Spread pear mixture into 4 individual ceramic moulds, spoon topping over each and bake for 20–30 minutes or until firm to the touch. Serve at room temperature with double cream.

TO MAKE TOPPING In a blender, cream butter, sugar and vanilla bean seeds. Add egg yolks, flour, milk and grappa. Blend until smooth. In a bowl, whisk egg whites and salt until they hold soft peaks. Fold whites into batter and spoon over pear mixture in ceramic moulds.

SERVES 4

cantucci al cioccolato
CHOCOLATE BISCOTTI

350 g blanched almonds
325 g (1⅓ cup) caster sugar
90 g (¾ cup) cocoa powder
300 g plain flour
1 tsp baking powder
Zest of 2 lemons
Zest of 2 oranges
3 whole eggs

Preheat oven to 175°C. Blend 150 g of the almonds with the sugar and cocoa powder until very finely processed. Chop the rest of the almonds roughly with a large knife. Mix all ingredients in a large bowl, roll into 6 large logs, place on baking trays and bake for 20 minutes at 175°C. Remove from oven, leave to cool slightly, then with a sharp knife cut diagonally into 1-cm slices. Reduce oven to 120°C, return biscotti to oven and bake for a further 5 minutes. (Makes approximately 60 biscuits.)

Robert Jacks,
Totem — Sketches of Spain,
1998, bronze

crostata di ricotta e rabarbaro
RHUBARB AND RICOTTA TART

1 quantity Short Sweet Pastry (see page 164)
20 stalks rhubarb
100 g caster sugar
30 ml (1 nip) grappa

TART Preheat oven to 175°C. Roll pastry out onto a floured surface until 6 mm thick. Ease pastry into a fluted 28-cm wide by 4-cm deep pastry tin. Refrigerate for 20 minutes before cooking. Blind bake the tart until pale golden (about 15 minutes).

Wash the rhubarb and cut the stalks into 3-cm lengths. Combine with caster sugar and grappa in a stainless steel pan and cook over low heat until the rhubarb is tender but still holds its shape. Remove from heat and allow to cool. When cool, spread rhubarb into baked pastry shell, then pour ricotta topping mixture over the top. Bake at 150°C for 20–25 minutes. Serve at room temperature.

TOPPING
250 g ricotta
2 eggs
110 g caster sugar
½ cup mascarpone cheese

Place all ingredients into a blender and purée until smooth.

SERVES 8

Salvatore Zofrea, *Woman Vase*, 1989

crostatina di rabarbaro, zabaione e zucchero bruciato
TARTLET OF RHUBARB, COLD ZABAIONE AND GLAZED SUGAR

1 quantity Short Sweet Pastry (see page 164)
12 stalks of rhubarb
60 g (¼ cup) caster sugar
20 ml lemon juice

COLD ZABAIONE
4 egg yolks
60 g (¼ cup) caster sugar
60 ml (¼ cup) dry marsala
¼ cup whipped cream
Icing sugar for glaze

Preheat oven to 175°C. Roll pastry out onto a floured surface until 6 mm thick. Ease pastry into 8 fluted 8-cm wide by 4-cm deep pastry tins. Refrigerate for 20 minutes before cooking. Blind bake the tarts until pale golden (about 15 minutes).

Wash the rhubarb and cut the stalks into 3-cm lengths. Combine with caster sugar and lemon juice in a stainless steel pan and cook over low heat until the rhubarb is tender but still holds its shape. Remove from heat and allow to cool. When cool, spread rhubarb into baked pastry shells, then spoon cold zabaione over the top. Sprinkle icing sugar generously over the top of the tarts, then glaze under a hot grill for 2 minutes.

TO MAKE COLD ZABAIONE In a wide, shallow pan, whisk egg yolks, caster sugar and marsala together. Place over a gentle, direct heat and continue whisking for 15 minutes or until the sabayon is cooked, light and fluffy. Remove from heat, place pan on a bowl of ice and whisk sabayon until cold. Fold in whipped cream.

CROSTATA DI RICOTTA E RABARBARO >   SERVES 8

gelato al miele
HONEY ICE CREAM

800 ml milk
12 egg yolks
150 g caster sugar

300 g clear honey
200 ml cream

In a heavy-based saucepan, bring milk to the boil. In a large bowl, whisk egg yolks and sugar for 2 minutes. Add hot milk, stirring gently. Return mixture to the saucepan and cook over low heat, stirring constantly, until mixture coats the back of a spoon. (Do not overcook, or you will end up with scrambled eggs.) Remove from heat and strain through a fine sieve. Cool slightly, then add honey and cream. Cool completely over ice. When cold, churn in an ice cream machine, then freeze.

SERVES 10

ABOVE: John Beard, *The Beautiful and the Damned I*, 1993, acrylic on paper

OPPOSITE: John Beard, *The Beautiful and the Damned II*, 1993, acrylic on paper

gelato alla vaniglia
VANILLA ICE CREAM

500 ml milk
500 ml cream
4 vanilla beans, split

16 egg yolks
300 g caster sugar

In a heavy-based saucepan, bring milk, cream and vanilla beans to the boil. In a large bowl, whisk egg yolks and sugar for 2 minutes. Add hot cream and milk, stirring gently. Return mixture to the saucepan and cook over low heat, stirring constantly, until mixture coats the back of a spoon. (Do not overcook, or you will end up with scrambled eggs.) Remove from heat and strain through a fine sieve. Cool mixture down over ice. When cold, churn in an ice cream machine, then freeze.

SERVES 10

panforte
PANFORTE

215 g mixed peel
185 g hazelnut kernels, roughly chopped
90 g blanched almonds
¾ tsp cinnamon powder
¼ tsp nutmeg

3 pinches white pepper
60 g (½ cup) plain flour
125 g (½ cup) caster sugar
125 g honey

Preheat oven to 150°C. Line a 30-cm by 15-cm tray with greaseproof paper. In a large bowl, combine mixed peel and all dry ingredients, mix well and set aside.

In a heavy-based saucepan, combine sugar and honey and bring to the boil. Cook the mixture until it registers 125°C on a sugar thermometer. Pour sugar syrup onto the dry ingredients and stir well. Spoon evenly into the lined tray and flatten with wet hands if necessary. The cake should be about 2 cm thick. Bake for about 45 minutes at 150°C. The panforte will seem underdone, but it will harden as it cools. Cool completely in the tray and then invert onto a platter. Slice into bite-sized pieces.

SERVES 10

NOTE Panforte will keep for up to 2 weeks in the refrigerator.

pere cotte con sorbetto di pere e cantucci
POACHED PEARS WITH PEAR SORBET AND CHOCOLATE BISCOTTI

6 pears
500 ml Moscato (dessert wine)
200 g caster sugar
1 vanilla bean, split
Chocolate Biscotti (see page 167), to
  serve

SORBET
200 g pears
Juice of 1 lemon
100 ml water
100 g caster sugar

Peel pears and split them in half from top to bottom. Remove stalks and seeds with a small knife. Place pears, Moscato, sugar and vanilla bean in a saucepan and bring to the boil. Reduce heat and simmer for 10 minutes. Leave pears to cool in syrup.

To serve, slice pears and arrange on a serving plate with pear sorbet and chocolate biscotti.

TO MAKE SORBET Peel, seed and chop pears and place in a stainless steel saucepan with lemon juice, water and sugar. Bring to the boil, reduce the heat and simmer for 15 minutes. Remove pears, reserving the cooking liquid. Process pears in an upright blender until smooth. Place in a bowl with the cooking liquid and leave to cool completely. When cold, churn in an ice cream machine, then freeze.

SERVES 6

Michael Johnson, Ceramic plate, 1998

rotolo al limone con gelato al miele
LEMON ROULADE WITH HONEY ICE CREAM

SPONGE
6 egg yolks
200 g icing sugar, sieved
8 egg whites
100 g almond meal
4 tsp cornflour
1 quantity Honey Ice Cream (see
  page 171), to serve

FILLING
200 g sour cream
Zest of 2 lemons
Juice of 1 lemon
80 g caster sugar

Whisk egg yolks and 110 g of the icing sugar for 6 minutes until light and thick. Whisk egg whites until they become opaque, add the remaining icing sugar and beat until whites are stiff. Fold one-quarter of the egg white into the egg yolks. Add almond meal and cornflour, then fold in the remaining three-quarters of the egg white. Spoon into a greased 30-cm by 20-cm tray and bake at 180°C for 8–10 minutes. When cooked, invert onto a cloth and leave to cool. Once sponge is cool, spread filling evenly over the sponge, roll up the sponge, using the cloth, and refrigerate for 1 hour before serving.

To serve, remove from the cloth, slice roulade and arrange on serving plates with honey ice cream. The roulade can also be served with poached fruits.

TO MAKE FILLING Mix all the ingredients in a bowl.

SERVES 8

PERE COTTE CON SORBETTO DI PERE E CANTUCCI >

Charles Blackman, *Alice's Feast*, oil on canvas

semifreddo al caffé
COFFEE SEMIFREDDO WITH PRALINE

SEMIFREDDO
4 egg yolks
60 ml (2 nips) coffee liqueur
150 g caster sugar
2 egg whites
300 ml whipped cream
1 tblsp fresh coffee, finely ground

PRALINE
125 g hazelnuts
125 g almonds
1 egg white
100 g caster sugar

In a wide, shallow pan, combine egg yolks, coffee liqueur and half the caster sugar and whisk together over a double boiler. Continue to whisk until cooked (7–8 minutes). Set aside and allow to cool.

In a large bowl, whisk egg whites until they become opaque, then rain in the remaining sugar and beat until whites are stiff. Fold whipped cream into cold sabayon, add ground coffee and then fold in whisked egg whites. Place into 7 180-ml Dariole moulds and freeze for 30–40 minutes.

To serve, dip semifreddo moulds into hot water for 5 seconds then invert onto serving plates. The ice cream will slip straight out. Serve with crushed praline.

TO MAKE PRALINE Mix all ingredients together in a bowl. Place on a greased tray and bake for 20–30 minutes at 175°C. The edges may cook first, so stir the mixture every 5 minutes while it is cooking. Remove from oven, allow to cool completely, then crush.

SERVES 7

spuma di mascarpone
MASCARPONE MOUSSE

200 g mascarpone cheese
3 eggs, separated
100 g sugar
80 g dark chocolate, in small pieces
8 Amaretti biscuits
60 ml (2 nips) Amaretto liqueur

In a bowl, combine the mascarpone and the egg yolks and beat until smooth. In another bowl, beat the egg whites and sugar until soft peaks form, then gently fold into the mascarpone mixture. Add the chocolate pieces and mix gently.

Line 4 small souffle dishes with liqueur-soaked Amaretti biscuits, then pour the mascarpone mixture on top. Serve cold.

SERVES 4

NOTE Instead of biscuits, you can use fresh berries, omitting the liqueur.

torta al cioccolato con fragole cotte
PRESSED CHOCOLATE CAKE WITH BAKED STRAWBERRIES

300 g butter
400 g dark chocolate
10 egg yolks
200 g caster sugar
4 tblsp cocoa powder
8 egg whites
Vanilla Ice Cream (see page 171), to serve

Melt butter and chocolate in the microwave or over a double boiler if you do not have a microwave, allow to cool slightly, then mix in the egg yolks, sugar and cocoa powder.

In a large bowl, whisk egg whites until stiff. Fold egg whites into chocolate mixture. Spoon into a 20-cm wide by 8-cm high springform tin. Bake at 180°C for 30–40 minutes. (The cake will still feel undercooked.) Place a light weight on top (for example, 2 plates) and allow to cool.

To serve, slice chocolate cake, arrange on plates with baked strawberries and a little of the cooking juices. Serve with vanilla ice cream.

BAKED STRAWBERRIES
2 punnets strawberries
50 g icing sugar, sieved
Juice of 1 lemon

Place strawberries, icing sugar and lemon juice in an ovenware dish and bake in preheated oven for 10 minutes at 160°C.

SERVES 6

Brian Seidel, *Mask*, 1997

torta di mascarpone e arancio
ORANGE AND MASCARPONE CAKE

CAKE
2 oranges
5 whole eggs
200 g almonds
200 g caster sugar
1 tsp baking soda

Cover oranges with water and boil for 40 minutes. Drain, cut into pieces and discard any seeds. Blend in a Robot Coupe (mixmaster) until finely puréed. Add eggs, almonds, sugar and baking soda. Pour into a 20-cm wide by 8-cm high springform tin and bake for 20–30 minutes at 175°C. Remove from oven and allow to cool completely before removing from tin.

To assemble, slice cake crossways into four layers. Return one layer to the springform tin and spread some of the mascarpone on top. Continue to layer cake and mascarpone, finishing with a cake layer. Refrigerate for 30 minutes, then serve with orange and cardamom sauce.

MASCARPONE
2 whole eggs
80 g caster sugar
500 g mascarpone cheese

In a large bowl, whisk eggs and sugar until sugar has dissolved. Fold in the mascarpone cheese (you may have to whisk again depending on the mascarpone).

ORANGE AND CARDAMOM SAUCE
Juice of 4 oranges
80 g caster sugar
1 tsp cardamom seeds

Place orange juice into a saucepan with sugar and bring to the boil. Reduce heat and simmer until semi-thick. Add cardamom seeds and leave to cool completely.

SERVES 6

Charles Blackman,
Pen on napkin done
at the table, 1989

index

JOHN OLSEN AND LUCIO GALLETTO

Page numbers in bold, e.g. **26**, refer to recipes.
Page numbers in italics, e.g. *27*, refer to illustrations.

JOHN COBURN AND FRED CRESS

TIM STORRIER AND GARRY SHEAD

FRED CRESS, JOHN BEARD AND TIM STORRIER

GARRY SHEAD, TOM LOWENSTEIN AND JOHN OLSEN

acknowledgments

I would like to thank:

Deborah Hart, for having the idea.

Nevill and Anna Drury, for believing in us.

Leo Schofield, for his support and extraordinary research and finding the time to write the foreword.

John Olsen, who is very dear to me, for understanding my philosophy about food without need of words.

Robert Hughes, for gracing the introductory pages of this book with his wonderful prose.

David Dale, for his passion for all things Italian and his contribution to the book.

All my artist friends, for participating so willingly and enthusiastically in this project.

Our discerning clientele.

All the staff at Lucio's, past and present.

Paul Green, for his remarkable photography and patience.

Marah Braye and Caroline de Fries at Craftsman House, for their enthusiasm and dedication.

My family in Italy.

My very good friend, Armando Percuoco, for the many years of encouragement.

My wife, Sally, and my two children, Matteo and Michela, for being my best critics.

A special thanks to Andrew Berry and the current team in the kitchen.

Timothy and I would also like to thank each other.

ABOVE: Carlo Montesi, Pencil drawings, 1990

Distributed in Australia by Craftsman House,
Tower A, 112 Talavera Road,
North Ryde, Sydney, NSW 2113
in association with G+B Arts International:
Australia, Canada, France, Germany, India,
Japan, Luxembourg, Malaysia, The Netherlands,
Russia, Singapore, Switzerland

ISBN 90 5703 332 1

DESIGN: Caroline de Fries
PHOTOGRAPHY: Paul Green
INDEX: Alan Walker
COLOUR SEPARATIONS: Chroma Graphics, Singapore
PRINTER: Kyodo Printing Co., Singapore

PAGE 1: Fred Cress, Ceramic plate, 1998
PAGE 2: Salvatore Zofrea, *Untitled*, 1998, watercolour
PAGE 4: John Olsen, Menu cover, 1997